P9-DNA-547

The Essential
BERNIE
SANDERS
and his
Vision for America

The Essential

BERNIE SANDERS

and his
Vision for America

Jonathan
Tasini

Chelsea Green Publishing
White River Junction, Vermont

Copyright © 2015 by Jonathan Tasini.
All rights reserved.

No part of this book may be transmitted or
reproduced in any form by any means without
permission in writing from the publisher.

Project Manager: Patricia Stone
Project Editor: Shay Totten
Copy Editor: Laura Jorstad
Proofreader: Angela Boyle
Indexer: Shana Milkie
Designer: Melissa Jacobson

Printed in the United States of America by Thomson-Shore,
a 100 percent employee-owned company.

First printing August 2015.
10 9 8 7 6 5 4 3 2 1   15 16 17 18

Our Commitment to Green Publishing
Chelsea Green sees publishing as a tool for cultural change and ecological stewardship. We
strive to align our book manufacturing practices with our editorial mission and to reduce
the impact of our business enterprise in the environment. We print our books and catalogs
on chlorine-free recycled paper, using vegetable-based inks whenever possible. This book
may cost slightly more because it was printed on paper that contains recycled fiber, and we
hope you'll agree that it's worth it. Chelsea Green is a member of the Green Press Initiative
(www.greenpressinitiative.org), a nonprofit coalition of publishers, manufacturers, and
authors working to protect the world's endangered forests and conserve natural resources.
The Essential Bernie Sanders and His Vision for America was printed on paper supplied by
Thomson-Shore that contains 100% postconsumer recycled fiber.

Library of Congress Cataloging-in-Publication Data is available upon request.

Chelsea Green Publishing
85 North Main Street, Suite 120
White River Junction, VT 05001
(802) 295-6300
www.chelseagreen.com

For my parents,
and for Donna Parson, who spent a lifetime
mentoring and encouraging countless people
who are building a progressive world. She
walked the walk every day.

PROPERTY OF
LIBRARY OF THE CHATHAMS
CHATHAM NJ

Contents

Preface

I've been involved in politics my whole life, from stuffing envelopes to knocking on doors in all kinds of weather to working closely with politicians. So my bullshit alarm is on a hair-trigger alert in the presence of most politicians—and it goes off with regularity, even among those I agree with.

A couple of years ago, something different happened. Over the course of a couple of days in 2013, I spent a number of hours chatting with Bernie Sanders for an interview for *Playboy*. To be sure, it was a pleasure—unfortunately, too rare an experience—to be with a member of Congress who actually had an informed, complex understanding of the issues facing the people. It's a deep understanding steeped in a worldview that seeks to represent the regular person, not because it tests well in polls but because Bernie believes what he says.

When I walked out of Bernie Sanders' office, aside from the energy one feels from a good policy give-and-take, I was left with an unusually strong sense of something else: **authenticity**.

Authenticity is hard to manufacture—and as we all know, politicians of all stripes spend many hours and millions of dollars to painfully, and often comically, try to say to voters, "I'm like you; I'm real."

But authenticity is easy to explain. It's a simple sense: "Here it is. Here is what I believe from deep inside. I don't need to convene a think-a-thon of consultants and other sycophants to tell me what I should believe. This is me."

That is the essence of Bernie Sanders. No bullshit. Unvarnished opinions and beliefs.

Now Bernie carries that authenticity into the national arena in his quest to become president of the United States. As I write these words, tens of thousands of people have already swarmed to hear him speak the truth at mass rallies in arenas and halls across the nation.

To be clear: This is an *electorally successful* politician, elected mayor of Burlington, Vermont (as an independent), four times beginning in 1981, serving as the state's lone member in the US House of Representatives from 1990 to 2006, and finally, in 2006, ascending to the US Senate.

Which elicits a question some have asked about his inspiring campaign for the White House: Why is the longest-serving independent in Congress, who describes himself without hesitation as a Democratic Socialist, running for president in the Democratic Party primaries?

To be sure, some of it is practical. Unless you are a billionaire, it's virtually impossible to win a national election as an independent in the dominant two-party system (and even, as Ross Perot proved, being a billionaire does not make it a cinch). Some of it has to do with branding and the corrupted nature of Super-PAC-fueled elections in the post–*Citizens United* world, a topic Bernie feels passionately about, as you will read in this book.

But there is something more here. In an exchange we had back in 2013, I asked Bernie whether he thinks people understand the term *class warfare*, which is at the heart of his orations about how the historic divide between rich and poor is ripping apart the nation.

He replied: "Sometimes people come up to me and say I'm courageous for saying all these things. I say, 'I'm not courageous. Go look at these guys who want to give more tax breaks to billionaires and cut programs for working families. That is incredibly courageous because the vast majority of the American people think that's crazy.' The polling says: Don't cut Social Security; don't cut Medicare; don't cut Medicaid. Ask the wealthy and large corporations to pay more taxes. The political question is, why have the Republicans not been reduced to a 15 percent marginal third party? [The answer is] most people do not perceive a heck of a lot of difference between either party. The Democrats are too diffuse, and their message is so unclear the American people don't see the real difference."

This is the essence of his belief that he can win: He is certain that if he speaks boldly, clearly, honestly, and authentically, he can win the Democratic nomination for president, and the party he leads can win everywhere—in all fifty states—and relegate a regressive anti-worker, pro-corporate Republican Party to rump status. It would be a party transformed, with a standard-bearer who would not hesitate to say exactly what he believes, as this book lays out, whether he is walking the streets of Newark, Tampa, Eugene, Detroit, or Dallas, trekking from the Deep South to the Midwest, or traveling from sea to shining sea.

The goal of this book is to present to the country, in a succinct way, Bernie's authenticity and his accomplishments, a vision that he believes is a winning agenda because it exactly reflects, whatever labels one sticks on the messenger, the desires and beliefs of a majority of people. No one should underestimate—and Bernie does not—the challenge of winning the White House; it is a steep climb for a whole set of logistical and organizational reasons.

But what is laid out here is a simple point: His path to victory is possible because, in his authenticity, his views are America's views.

Bernie Sanders carries with him a hope and vision for a twenty-first-century caring, sustainable, more just and fair United States of America.

I aimed to be brief. Each chapter is short. Each chapter can be read on its own, depending on a reader's interest. I've used Bernie's direct words, mostly from speeches on the floor of the Senate or House or in statements he's made, because he usually does so with very concrete explanations and descriptions of a problem that any reader can follow. Each chapter has my own short introduction to give some background and ends with specific steps Bernie has taken to implement his views.

It's important to underscore a point from the title of the book. This is what I think are the *essential* views of Bernie Sanders—not the *complete* views. I wanted this book out fast, as a handy organizing tool. It allows readers to reach conclusions about Bernie's worldview and overall philosophy, and to seek out additional positions on other issues not covered in the chapters.

Hopefully, the words presented here will help individuals make the argument for Bernie's candidacy to a family member, neighbor, friend, or coworker.

But ultimately, as Bernie often says, this is not about him. It's about our chance to ignite a political revolution by exercising collective power to restore democracy and justice.

Feel the Bern.

—JONATHAN TASINI

Introduction

Bernie has been a tireless advocate for children, pushing for funding and legislation that supports the basic needs of working families and their children. He understands, unlike many politicians, the cost of heating fuel in the home, and gasoline in the car, the cost of child care and college tuition.

—Donna Bailey, executive director, Addison County Parent/Child Center, Middlebury, Vermont[1]

There's no leader Vermonters have ever respected and voted for quite the way they respect Bernie because they know that he always means what he says, and he always stands for what he believes.

—Bill McKibben, Vermont environmental activist and author[2]

On May 26, 2015, on a beautiful day in Burlington, Vermont, Senator Bernie Sanders announced his campaign for president before thousands of cheering supporters. He had spent many months weighing whether to enter the race, consulting with people across the country. To many he would say that he cherished the position he currently held, from which he could serve the interests of the people of Vermont. He would also say that he didn't wake up every day with an unstoppable desire to be president of the United States.

But with full understanding of the financial and physical challenge a nationwide presidential race entails, he also recognized that the country is in crisis. He believes this is a singular moment because people across the political spectrum, in every state, are yearning for solutions that address the historic gap between rich and poor and because both political parties have failed to provide leadership that place people first.

Here is the full text of his announcement, which gives the broad overview of his vision of a political revolution—an overview that the rest of this book breaks down into more detail.   —J.T.

Thank you all very much for being here and for all the support that you have given me over the years: as the mayor of this great city, as Vermont's only congressman and now as a U.S. senator. Thanks also to my longtime friends and fellow Vermonters Bill McKibben, Brenda Torpey, Donna Bailey, Mike O'Day and Ben [Cohen] and Jerry [Greenfield] for all that you do—and for your very generous remarks. Thanks also to Jenny Nelson for moderating this event and for your leadership in Vermont agriculture.

I also want to thank my family: My wife Jane, my brother Larry, my children Levi, Heather, Carina and Dave for their love and support, and my seven beautiful grandchildren—Sonny, Cole, Ryleigh, Grayson, Ella, Tess and Dylan who provide so much joy in my life.

Today, here in our small state—a state that has led the nation in so many ways—I am proud to announce my candidacy for president of the United States of America.

Today, with your support and the support of millions of people throughout this country, we begin a political revolution to transform our country economically, politically, socially and environmentally.

Today, we stand here and say loudly and clearly that; "Enough is enough. This great nation and its government belong to all of the people, and not to a handful of billionaires, their Super-PACs and their lobbyists."

Brothers and sisters: Now is not the time for thinking small. Now is not the time for the same old–same old establishment politics and stale inside-the-beltway ideas.

Now is the time for millions of working families to come together, to revitalize American democracy, to end the collapse of the American middle class and to make certain that our children and grandchildren are able to enjoy a quality of life that brings them health, prosperity, security and joy—and that once again makes the

United States the leader in the world in the fight for economic and social justice, for environmental sanity and for a world of peace.

My fellow Americans: This country faces more serious problems today than at any time since the Great Depression and, if you include the planetary crisis of climate change, it may well be that the challenges we face now are direr than any time in our modern history.

Here is my promise to you for this campaign. Not only will I fight to protect the working families of this country, but we're going to build a movement of millions of Americans who are prepared to stand up and fight back. We're going to take this campaign directly to the people—in town meetings, at door-to-door conversations, on street corners and in social media—and that's BernieSanders.com by the way. This week we will be in New Hampshire, Iowa and Minnesota—and that's just the start of a vigorous grassroots campaign.

Let's be clear. This campaign is not about Bernie Sanders. It is not about Hillary Clinton. It is not about Jeb Bush or anyone else. This campaign is about the needs of the American people, and the ideas and proposals that effectively address those needs. As someone who has never run a negative political ad in his life, my campaign will be driven by issues and serious debate; not political gossip, not reckless personal attacks or character assassination. This is what I believe the American people want and deserve. I hope other candidates agree, and I hope the media allows that to happen. Politics in a democratic society should not be treated like a baseball game, a game show or a soap opera. The times are too serious for that.

Let me take a minute to touch on some of the issues that I will be focusing on in the coming months, and then give you an outline of an Agenda for America which will, in fact, deal with these problems and lead us to a better future.

Income and Wealth Inequality: Today, we live in the wealthiest nation in the history of the world but that reality means very little for most of us because almost all of that wealth is owned and controlled by a tiny handful of individuals. In America we now have more income and wealth inequality than any other major country on earth, and the gap between the very rich and everyone is wider than at any time since the 1920s. The issue of wealth and income inequality is the great moral issue of our time, it is the great economic issue of our time and it is the great political issue of our time. And we will address it.

Let me be very clear. There is something profoundly wrong when the top one-tenth of 1 percent owns almost as much wealth as the bottom 90 percent, and when 99 percent of all new income goes to the top 1 percent. There is something profoundly wrong when, in recent years, we have seen a proliferation of millionaires and billionaires at the same time as millions of Americans work longer hours for lower wages and we have the highest rate of childhood poverty of any major country on earth. There is something profoundly wrong when one family owns more wealth than the bottom 130 million Americans. This grotesque level of inequality is immoral. It is bad economics. It is unsustainable. This type of rigged economy is not what America is supposed to be about. This has got to change and, as your president, together we will change it.

Economics: But it is not just income and wealth inequality. It is the tragic reality that for the last 40 years the great middle class of our country—once the envy of the world—has been disappearing. Despite exploding technology and increased worker productivity, median family income is almost $5,000 less than it was in 1999. In Vermont and throughout this country it is not uncommon for people to be working two or three jobs just to cobble together enough income to survive on and some health care benefits.

The truth is that real unemployment is not the 5.4 percent you read in newspapers. It is close to 11 percent if you include those workers who have given up looking for jobs or who are working part time when they want to work full time. Youth unemployment is over 17 percent and African American youth unemployment is much higher than that. Today, shamefully, we have 45 million people living in poverty, many of whom are working at low-wage jobs. These are the people who struggle every day to find the money to feed their kids, to pay their electric bills and to put gas in the car to get to work. This campaign is about those people and our struggling middle class. It is about creating an economy that works for all, and not just the one percent.

***Citizens United*:** My fellow Americans: Let me be as blunt as I can and tell you what you already know. As a result of the disastrous Supreme Court decision on *Citizens United*, the American political system has been totally corrupted, and the foundations of American democracy are being undermined. What the Supreme Court essentially said was that it was not good enough for the billionaire class to own much of our economy. They could now own the U.S. government as well. And that is precisely what they are trying to do.

American democracy is not about billionaires being able to buy candidates and elections. It is not about the Koch brothers, Sheldon Adelson and other incredibly wealthy individuals spending billions of dollars to elect candidates who will make the rich richer and everyone else poorer. According to media reports the Koch brothers alone, one family, will spend more money in this election cycle than either the Democratic or Republican parties. This is not democracy. This is oligarchy. In Vermont and at our town meetings we know what American democracy is supposed to be about. It is one person, one vote—with every citizen having an equal say—and no voter suppression. And that's the kind of American political system we have to fight for and will fight for in this campaign.

Climate Change: When we talk about our responsibilities as human beings and as parents, there is nothing more important than leaving this country and the entire planet in a way that is habitable for our kids and grandchildren. The debate is over. The scientific community has spoken in a virtually unanimous voice. Climate change is real. It is caused by human activity and it is already causing devastating problems in the United States and around the world.

The scientists are telling us that if we do not boldly transform our energy system away from fossil fuels and into energy efficiency and sustainable energies, this planet could be five to ten degrees Fahrenheit warmer by the end of this century. This is catastrophic. It will mean more drought, more famine, more rising sea level, more floods, more ocean acidification, more extreme weather disturbances, more disease and more human suffering. We must not, we cannot, and we will not allow that to happen.

It is no secret that there is massive discontent with politics in America today. In the mid-term election in November, 63 percent of Americans did not vote, including 80 percent of young people. Poll after poll tells us that our citizens no longer have confidence in our political institutions and, given the power of Big Money in the political process, they have serious doubts about how much their vote actually matters and whether politicians have any clue as to what is going on in their lives.

Combating this political alienation, this cynicism and this legitimate anger will not be easy. That's for sure. But that is exactly what, together, we have to do if we are going to turn this country around—and that is what this campaign is all about.

And to bring people together we need a simple and straight-forward progressive agenda which speaks to the needs of our people, and which provides us with a vision of a very different America. And what is that agenda?

Jobs, Jobs, Jobs: It begins with jobs. If we are truly serious about reversing the decline of the middle class we need a major federal jobs program which puts millions of Americans back to work at decent paying jobs. At a time when our roads, bridges, water systems, rail and airports are decaying, the most effective way to rapidly create meaningful jobs is to rebuild our crumbling infrastructure. That's why I've introduced legislation which would invest $1 trillion over 5 years to modernize our country's physical infrastructure. This legislation would create and maintain at least 13 million good-paying jobs, while making our country more productive, efficient and safe. And I promise you as president I will lead that legislation into law.

I will also continue to oppose our current trade policies. For decades, presidents from both parties have supported trade agreements which have cost us millions of decent paying jobs as corporate America shuts down plants here and moves to low-wage countries. As president, my trade policies will break that cycle of agreements which enrich at the expense of the working people of this country.

Raising Wages: Let us be honest and acknowledge that millions of Americans are now working for totally inadequate wages. The current federal minimum wage of $7.25 an hour is a starvation wage and must be raised. The minimum wage must become a living wage—which means raising it to $15 an hour over the next few years—which is exactly what Los Angeles recently did—and I applaud them for doing that. Our goal as a nation must be to ensure that no full-time worker lives in poverty. Further, we must establish pay equity for women workers. It's unconscionable that women earn 78 cents on the dollar compared to men who perform the same work. We must also end the scandal in which millions of American employees, often earning less than $30,000 a year, work 50 or 60 hours a week—and earn no overtime. And we need paid sick leave and guaranteed vacation time for all.

Addressing Wealth and Income Inequality: This campaign is going to send a message to the billionaire class. And that is: you can't have it all. You can't get huge tax breaks while children in this country go hungry. You can't continue sending our jobs to China while millions are looking for work. You can't hide your profits in the Cayman Islands and other tax havens, while there are massive unmet needs on every corner of this nation. Your greed has got to end. You cannot take advantage of all the benefits of America, if you refuse to accept your responsibilities.

That is why we need a tax system which is fair and progressive, which makes wealthy individuals and profitable corporations begin to pay their fair share of taxes.

Reforming Wall Street: It is time to break up the largest financial institutions in the country. Wall Street cannot continue to be an island unto itself, gambling trillions in risky financial instruments while expecting the public to bail it out. If a bank is too big to fail it is too big to exist. We need a banking system which is part of the job creating productive economy, not a handful of huge banks on Wall Street which engage in reckless and illegal activities.

Campaign Finance Reform: If we are serious about creating jobs, about climate change and the needs of our children and the elderly, we must be deadly serious about campaign finance reform and the need for a constitutional amendment to overturn *Citizens United*. I have said it before and I'll say it again. I will not nominate any justice to the Supreme Court who has not made it clear that he or she will move to overturn that disastrous decision which is undermining our democracy. Long term, we need to go further and establish public funding of elections.

Reversing Climate Change: The United States must lead the world in reversing climate change. We can do that if we transform our energy system away from fossil fuels, toward energy efficiency and such sustainable energies such as wind, solar, geo-thermal and bio-mass. Millions of homes and buildings need to be weatherized, our transportation system needs to be energy efficient, and we need a tax on carbon to accelerate the transition away from fossil fuel.

Health Care for All: The United States remains the only major country on earth that does not guarantee health care for all as a right. Despite the modest gains of the Affordable Care Act, 35 million Americans continue to lack health insurance and many more are under-insured. Yet, we continue paying far more per capita for health care than any other nation. The United States must join the rest of the industrialized world and guarantee health care to all as a right by moving toward a Medicare-for-All single-payer system.

Protecting Our Most Vulnerable: At a time when millions of Americans are struggling to keep their heads above water economically, at a time when senior poverty is increasing, at a time when millions of kids are living in dire poverty, my Republican colleagues, as part of their recently-passed budget, are trying to make a terrible situation even worse. If you can believe it, the Republican budget throws 27 million Americans off health insurance, makes drastic cuts in Medicare, throws millions of low-income Americans, including pregnant women off of nutrition programs, and makes it harder for working-class families to afford college or put their kids in the Head Start program. And then, to add insult to injury, they provide huge tax breaks for the very wealthiest families in this country while they raise taxes on working families.

Well, let me tell my Republican colleagues that I respectfully disagree with their approach. Instead of cutting Social Security, we're going to expand Social Security benefits. Instead of cutting Head Start and child care, we are going to move to a universal pre-K system for all the children of this country. As Franklin Delano Roosevelt reminded us, a nation's greatness is judged not by what it provides to the most well-off, but how it treats the people most in need. And that's the kind of nation we must become.

College for All: And when we talk about education, let me be very clear. In a highly competitive global economy, we need the best educated workforce we can create. It is insane and counter-productive to the best interests of our country, that hundreds of thousands of bright young people cannot afford to go to college, and that millions of others leave school with a mountain of debt that burdens them for decades. That must end. That is why, as president, I will fight to make tuition in public colleges and universities free, as well as substantially lower interest rates on student loans.

War and Peace: As everybody knows, we live in a difficult and dangerous world, and there are people out there who want to do us harm. As president, I will defend this nation—but I will do it responsibly. As a member of Congress I voted against the war in Iraq, and that was the right vote. I am vigorously opposed to an endless war in the Middle East—a war which is unwise and unnecessary. We must be vigorous in combating terrorism and defeating ISIS, but we should not have to bear that burden alone. We must be part of an international coalition, led by Muslim nations, that can not only defeat ISIS but begin the process of creating conditions for a lasting peace.

As some of you know, I was born in a far-away land called Brooklyn, New York. My father came to this country from Poland without a penny in his pocket and without much of an education. My mother graduated high school in New York City. My father worked for almost his entire life as a paint salesman and we were solidly lower-middle class. My parents, brother and I lived in a small rent-controlled apartment. My mother's dream was to move out of that small apartment into a home of our own. She died young and her dream was never fulfilled. As a kid I learned, in many, many ways, what lack of money means to a family. That's a lesson I have never forgotten.

I have seen the promise of America in my own life. My parents would have never dreamed that their son would be a U.S. Senator, let alone run for president. But for too many of our fellow Americans, the dream of progress and opportunity is being denied by the grind of an economy that funnels all the wealth to the top.

And to those who say we cannot restore the dream, I say just look where we are standing. This beautiful place was once an unsightly rail yard that served no public purpose and was an eyesore. As mayor, I worked with the people of Burlington to help turn this waterfront into the beautiful people-oriented public space it is today. We took the fight to the courts, to the legislature and to the people. And we won.

The lesson to be learned is that when people stand together, and are prepared to fight back, there is nothing that can't be accomplished.

We can live in a country:

- Where every person has health care as a right, not a privilege;
- Where every parent can have quality and affordable childcare and where all of our qualified young people, regardless of income, can go to college;
- Where every senior can live in dignity and security, and not be forced to choose between their medicine or their food;
- Where every veteran who defends this nation gets the quality health care and benefits they have earned and receives the respect they deserve;
- Where every person, no matter their race, their religion, their disability or their sexual orientation realizes the full promise of equality that is our birthright as Americans.

That is the nation we can build together, and I ask you to join me in this campaign to build a future that works for all of us, and not just the few on top.

Thank you, and on this beautiful day on the shore of Lake Champlain, I welcome you aboard.[3]

1

Economy

Ten Ways to Make It Work for Everyone

What a lot of people are feeling [about Sanders] is that there is somebody speaking to their issues. I think that's why you're seeing so many people come out. People are sick and tired of corporate America, both Republican and Democrat.

—Troy Jackson, a logger from Allagash and
former majority leader of the Maine Senate[4]

Everyone cares about how the government spends its money, especially people who embrace the idea that smart, progressive government is a force for good. From the time he was watching taxpayer money as mayor of Burlington right up through his service in the House and Senate, Bernie has always looked for the proper balance between, on the one hand, strong, effective programs that look out for the people and, on the other, financing those programs by asking people who earn more to pay their fair share.

Even before his current campaign for the White House, Bernie thought through, in ten easy steps, a plan to meet human needs by raising hundreds of billions of dollars from the wealthy and corporations, and by reducing wasteful spending. Not a single dime from the list below would come from working people. —J.T.

Ten Fair Ways to Reduce the Deficit and Create Jobs[5]

At a time when we are experiencing more wealth and income inequality than at any time since the 1920s, and when Wall Street and large corporations are enjoying record breaking profits, I believe that we should be asking the very wealthiest people in this country to start paying their fair share of taxes. That way, we will not only lower the deficit but we will bring in enough revenue to invest in our economy and create the millions of new jobs we desperately need.

From both a moral and economic perspective, we must not balance the budget on the elderly, the children, the sick, working families, and the most vulnerable.

Here are 10 examples of how we can raise revenue and reduce spending in a fair way.

1. **Stop corporations from using offshore tax havens to avoid U.S. taxes.** Each and every year, the United States loses an estimated $100 billion in tax revenues due to offshore tax abuses by the wealthy and large corporations. The situation has become so absurd that one five-story office building in the Cayman Islands is now the "home" to more than 18,000 corporations.

   The wealthy and large corporations should not be allowed to avoid paying taxes by setting up tax shelters in Panama, the Cayman Islands, Bermuda, the Bahamas or other tax haven countries. The first bill that I introduced in the Senate (the Corporate Tax Dodging Prevention Act) would raise more than $580 billion over the next decade by eliminating the most egregious corporate offshore tax haven abuses.

2. **Establish a Robin Hood tax on Wall Street speculators.** Both the economic crisis and the deficit crisis are a direct result of the greed and recklessness on Wall Street. Creating a speculation fee of just 0.03 percent on the sale of credit default swaps, derivatives, options, futures, and large amounts of stock would reduce gambling on Wall Street, encourage the financial sector to invest in the job-creating productive economy, and reduce the deficit by $352 billion over 10 years, according to the Joint Committee on Taxation.

3. **End tax breaks and subsidies for big oil, gas and coal companies.** If we ended tax breaks and subsidies for big oil, gas, and coal companies, we could reduce the deficit by more than $113 billion over the next ten years. The five largest oil companies in the United States have made over $1 trillion

in profits over the past decade. ExxonMobil is now the most profitable corporation in the world. Large, profitable fossil fuel companies do not need a tax break.

4. **Establish a Progressive Estate Tax.** If we established a progressive estate tax on inherited wealth of more than $3.5 million, we could raise more than $300 billion over 10 years. [I] introduced the Responsible Estate Tax Act that would reduce the deficit in a fair way while ensuring that 99.7 percent of Americans would never pay a penny in estate taxes.

5. **Tax capital gains and dividends the same as work.** Taxing capital gains and dividends the same way that we tax work would raise more than $500 billion over the next decade. Warren Buffett has often said that he pays a lower effective tax rate than his secretary. The reason for this is that the wealthy obtain most of their income from capital gains and dividends, which is taxed at a much lower rate than work. Right now, the top marginal income tax for working is 39.6%, but the top tax rate on corporate dividends and capital gains is only 23.9%.

6. **Repeal all of the 2001 and 2003 Bush tax breaks for the top two percent.** In January, Congress finally repealed the Bush tax breaks for the top one percent—households making more than $450,000 a year. But the Bush tax breaks have been continued for the top two percent—households with incomes between $250,000 and $450,000 a year. Repealing the Bush tax breaks for all of the top two percent would reduce the deficit by about $400 billion over the next decade. After President Clinton increased taxes on the top two percent, the economy added over 22 million jobs. After President Bush reduced taxes for the rich, the economy lost over 600,000 private sector jobs.

7. **Eliminate the cap on taxable income that goes into the Social Security Trust Fund.** If we are serious about making sure that Social Security can pay all of the benefits owed to every eligible American for the next 50 to 75 years, we don't do that by cutting benefits, we do that by scrapping the cap on taxable income so

that a millionaire and a billionaire pay the same percentage of their income into Social Security as someone making $40,000 or $50,000 a year. Right now, someone who earns $113,700 a year pays the same amount of money in Social Security taxes as a billionaire. This makes no sense. Applying the Social Security payroll tax on income above $250,000 would ensure that Social Security remains solvent for the next 50 years. This plan would only impact the wealthiest 1.3 percent of wage earners; 98.7 percent of wage earners in the United States would not see their taxes go up by one dime.

8. **Establish a currency manipulation fee on China and other countries.** As almost everyone knows, China is manipulating its currency, giving it an unfair trade advantage over the United States and destroying decent paying manufacturing jobs in the process. If we imposed a currency manipulation fee on China and other currency manipulators, the Economic Policy Institute has estimated that we could raise $500 billion over 10 years and create 1 million jobs in the process.

9. **Reduce unnecessary and wasteful spending at the Pentagon,** which now consumes over half of our discretionary budget. Much of the huge spending at the Pentagon is devoted to spending money on Cold War weapons programs to fight a Soviet Union that no longer exists. Lawrence Korb, an Assistant Secretary of Defense under Ronald Reagan, has estimated that we could achieve significant savings of around $100 billion a year at the Pentagon while still ensuring that the United States has the strongest and most powerful military in the world.

10. **Require Medicare to negotiate for lower prescription drug prices with the pharmaceutical industry.** Requiring Medicare to negotiate drug prices, similarly to what the VA currently does, would save more than $240 billion over 10 years.

Bernie Facts

- Bernie is a longtime critic of wasteful Pentagon spending and is pushing to save taxpayer money by cutting tens of billions of dollars from the military budget.

- Bernie has been perhaps the Senate's most passionate voice for making sure corporations and the wealthy pay their fair share in taxes. The leading organizational advocate for fair taxes, Citizens for Tax Justice, says that in many cases Bernie "has been the lone voice in the Senate fighting for legislation that would ensure that corporations and the wealthy pay their fair share."

- As part of his advocacy for a sane health care system, Bernie wants to enable Medicare to negotiate lower prices for drugs—which would save the country tens of billions of dollars.

2

Health Care

A Right for All

There are many of us out here, barely holding onto health insurance. And there are more than a few who are taking the chance of living uninsured.

—Nancy S. Buck, Aurora, Colorado[6]

Bernie has supported a single-payer, Medicare-for-all health care system for several decades, including his years in the House. As he has pointed out many times, the efforts by the Clinton and Obama administrations to reform health care were insufficient because both efforts continued to give the insurance and drug industries huge profits and bankrupt millions of Americans.

Though he did not believe the Affordable Care Act ("Obamacare") went far enough, he pushed successfully to include $12.5 billion in the legislation to dramatically expand access to community health centers, allowing those centers to ramp up services such as primary care, dental care, low-cost prescription drugs, and mental health counseling for more than twenty-five million Americans.

When the US Supreme Court recently ruled to preserve the ACA's core framework, Bernie praised the decision: "The Supreme Court recognized the common-sense reading of the Affordable Care Act that Congress intended to help all eligible Americans obtain health insurance whether they get it through state or national exchanges. Access to affordable health care should not depend on where you live. At a time when the United States is the only major country on earth that doesn't guarantee health care to all Americans—and 35 million of our citizens today still lack insurance—it would have been an outrage to throw 6.4 million more people off health insurance. What the United States should do is join every other major nation and recognize that health care is a right of citizenship. A Medicare-for-all, single-payer system would provide better care at less cost for more Americans."[7]

In this 2009 Senate floor debate, Bernie makes the case for a national health care system and why a single-payer system makes the most sense—financially and morally.   —J.T.

Bernie's Senate floor statement during debate, December 16, 2009[8]

The day will come, although I recognize it is not today, when the Congress will have the courage to stand up to the private insurance companies and the drug companies and the medical equipment suppliers and all of those who profit and make billions of dollars every single year off of human sickness. On that day, when it comes—and it will come—the U.S. Congress will finally proclaim that health care is a right of all people and not just a privilege. And that day will come, as surely as I stand here today.

There are those who think that Medicare-for-all is some kind of a fringe idea—that there are just a few leftwing folks out there who think this is the way to go. But let me assure you that this is absolutely not the case. The single-payer concept has widespread support from diverse groups from diverse regions throughout the United States. In fact, in a 2007 AP/Yahoo poll, 65 percent of respondents said that the United States should adopt a universal health insurance program in which everyone is covered under a program like Medicare that is run by the Government and financed by taxpayers. . . .

Why is it that we need an entirely new approach for health care in this country? The answer is pretty obvious. Our current system, dominated by profit-making insurance companies, simply does not work. Yes, we have to confess, it does work for the insurance companies that make huge profits and provide their CEOs with extravagant compensation packages. Yes, it does work—and we saw how well it worked right here on the floor yesterday—for the pharmaceutical industry which year after year leads almost every other industry in profit while charging the American people by far—not even close—the highest prices in the world for prescription drugs.

So it works for the insurance companies. It works for the drug companies. It works for the medical equipment suppliers and the many other companies who are making billions of dollars off of our health care system. But it is not working for—in fact, it is a disaster for—ordinary Americans.

Today, 46 million people in our country have no health insurance and an even higher number of people are underinsured, with high deductibles or copayments. Today, as our primary health care system collapses, tens of millions of Americans do not have access to a doctor on a regular basis and, tragically, some 45,000 of our fellow Americans who do not have access to a doctor on a regular basis die every single year. That is 15 times more Americans who die of preventable diseases than were murdered in the horrific 9/11 attack against our country. That takes place every year: the preventable deaths of 45,000 people.

This is not acceptable. These horrific deaths are a manifestation of a collapsing system that needs fundamental change. . . .

A man from Swanton, VT, in the northern part of our State, wrote to me to tell me the story of his younger brother, a Vietnam veteran, who died three weeks after being diagnosed with colon cancer. At the time he was diagnosed, he had been laid off from his job and could not afford COBRA coverage. This is what his brother said:

> When he was in enough pain to see a doctor it was too late. He left a wife and two teenage sons in the prime of his life at 50 years old. The attending physician said that, if he had only sought treatment earlier, he would still be alive.

Horrifically, tragically, that same story is being told in every State in this country over and over again. If only he had gone to the doctor in time he could have lived, but he didn't have any health insurance. That should not be taking place in the United States of America in the year 2009.

Our health care disaster extends beyond even the thousands who die needlessly every single year. Many others suffer unnecessary disability—strokes that leave them paralyzed because they couldn't afford treatment for their high blood pressure, or amputations, blindness, or kidney failure from untreated diabetes. Infants are born disabled because their mothers couldn't get the kind of prenatal care that every mother should have, and millions with mental illness go without care every single day.

In a town in northern Vermont not far from where I live, a physician told me that one-third of the patients she treats are unable to pay for the prescription drugs she prescribes. Think about the insanity of that. We ask doctors to diagnose our illness, to help us out, she writes the prescription for the drug, and one-third of her patients cannot afford to fill that prescription. That is insane. That is a crumbling health care system. The reason people cannot afford to fill their prescription drugs is that our people, because of pharmaceutical industry greed, are forced to pay by far the highest prices in the world for prescription drugs. This is indefensible. There is nobody who can come to the floor of this Senate and tell me that makes one shred of sense.

The disintegration of our health care system causes not only unnecessary human pain, suffering, and death, but it is also an economic disaster. Talk to small businesses in Vermont, New Hampshire, any place in this country, and they tell you they cannot afford to invest in their companies and create new jobs because all of their profits are going to soaring health care costs—10, 15, 20 percent a year. Talk to the recently bankrupt General Motors and they will tell you that they spend more money per automobile on health care than they do on steel. GM is forced to pay $1,500 per car on health care while Mercedes in Germany spends $419, and Toyota in Japan spends $97. Try to compete against that.

From an individual economic perspective, it is literally beyond comprehension that of the nearly 1 million people who will file for bankruptcy this year, the vast majority are filing for bankruptcy because of medically related illnesses. Let's take a deep breath and think about this from an emotional point of view. Let's think about the millions of people who are today struggling with cancer, struggling with heart disease, struggling with diabetes or other chronic illnesses. They are not even able to focus on their disease and trying to get well. They are summoning half their energy to fight with the insurance companies to make sure they get the coverage they need. That is not civilized. That is not worthy of the United States of America.

In my State of Vermont—and I suspect it is similar in New Hampshire and every other State—I have many times walked into small mom-and-pop stores and seen those little donation jars that say: Help out this or that family because the breadwinner is struggling with cancer and does not have any health insurance or little Sally needs some kind of operation and she doesn't have any health insurance, put in a buck or five bucks to help that family get the health care they need. This is the United States of America. This should and cannot be allowed to continue. . . .

Today, the United States spends almost twice as much per person on health care as any other country. Despite that, we have 46 million uninsured and many more underinsured and our health care outcomes are, in many respects—not all but in many respects—worse than other countries. Other countries, for example, have longer life expectancies than we do. They are better on infant mortality, and they do a lot better job in terms of preventable deaths. At the very beginning of this debate, we should have asked a very simple question: Why is it we are spending almost twice as much per person on health care as any other country with outcomes that, in many respects, are not as good?

According to an OECD report in 2007, the United States spent $7,290, over $7,000 per person on health care. Canada spent $3,895, almost half what we spent. France spent $3,601, less than half what we spent. The United Kingdom spent less than $3,000, and Italy spent $2,600 compared to the more than $7,000 we spent. Don't you think that maybe the first question we might have asked is: Why is it we spend so much and yet our health care outcomes, in many respects, are worse than other countries?

Why is it that that happens?

Let me tell you what other people will not tell you. One key issue that needed to be debated in this health care discussion has not been discussed. The simple reason as to why we spend so much more than any other country with outcomes that are not as good as many other countries is that this legislation, from the very beginning, started with the assumption that we need to maintain the private for-profit health insurance companies. That basic reality that we cannot touch private insurance companies, in fact that we have to dump millions more people into private health insurance companies, that was an issue that could not even be discussed. And as a result, despite all the money we spend, we get poor value for our investment.

According to the World Health Organization, the United States ranks 37th in terms of health system performance compared with other countries including: Australia, Canada, Germany, New Zealand, and the United Kingdom. The U.S. health system ranks less or less than half.

Sometimes these groups poll people. They go around the world and they poll people and they ask: How do you feel about your own health care system? We end up way down below other countries. Recently, while the Canadian health care system was being attacked every single day, they did a poll in Canada. They said to the Canadian people: What do you think about your health care system? People in America say you have a terrible system. Do you want to junk your system and adopt the American system?

By overwhelming numbers, the people of Canada said: Thank you, no thank you. We know the American system. We will stay with our system.

I was in the United Kingdom a couple months ago. I had an interesting experience. It was a Parliamentarian meeting. I met with a number of people in the Conservative Party—not the liberal Democratic Party, not the Labour Party, the Conservative Party, the party which likely will become the government of that country. The Conservatives were outraged by the kind of attacks being leveled against the national health system in their country, the lies we are being told about their system. In fact, the leader of the Conservative Party got up to defend the national health system in the United Kingdom and said: If we come to power, we will defend the national health system. Those were the conservatives.

What is the problem with our system, which makes it radically different than systems in any other industrialized country? It is that we have allowed for-profit private corporations to develop and run our health care system, and the system that these companies have developed is the most costly, wasteful, complicated, and bureaucratic in the entire world. Everybody knows that. With 1,300 private insurance companies and thousands and thousands of different health benefit programs all designed to maximize profits, private health insurance companies spend an incredible 30 percent of every health care dollar on administration and billing, on exorbitant CEO compensation packages, on advertising, lobbying, and campaign contributions. This amounts to some $350 billion every single year that is not spent on health care but is spent on wasteful bureaucracy.

It is spent on bureaucrats and on an insurance company telling us why we can't get the insurance we pay for. How many people are on the phone today arguing with those bureaucrats to try to get the benefits they paid for? It is spent on staff in a physician's office who spend all their time submitting claims. They are not treating people; they are submitting claims. It is spent on hundreds of people working in the basement of hospitals who are not delivering babies, not treating people with cancer. They are not making people well. They are sending out bills. That is the system we have decided to have. We send out bills, and we spend hundreds of billions of dollars doing that rather than bringing primary health care physicians into rural areas, rather than getting the doctors, dentists, and nurses we need. . . .

At a time when the middle class is collapsing and when millions of Americans are unable to afford health insurance, the profits of health insurance companies are soaring. From 2003 to 2007, the combined profits of the Nation's major health insurance companies increased by 170 percent. While more and more Americans are losing their jobs, the top executives of the industry are receiving lavish compensation packages. In 2007, despite plans to cut 3 to 4 percent of its workforce, Johnson & Johnson found the cash to pay its CEO Weldon $31.4 million. Ron Williams of Aetna took home over $38 million, and the head of CIGNA, Edward Hanway, took away $120 million over 5 years . . . and on and on it goes.

So what is the alternative?

Let me briefly describe the main features of a Medicare-for-all single-payer system. In terms of access, people getting into health care, this legislation would provide for all necessary medical care without cost sharing or other barriers to treatment. Every American—not 94 percent but 100 percent of America's citizens—would be entitled to care. In terms of choice, the issue is not choice of insurance companies that our Republican friends talk about. The question is choice of doctors, choice of hospitals, choice of therapeutic treatments. Our single-payer legislation would provide full choice of physicians and other licensed providers and hospitals. Importantly—and I know there is some confusion—a single-payer program is a national health insurance program which utilizes a nonprofit, private delivery system. It is not a government-run health care system. It is a government-run insurance program. In other words, people would still be going to the same doctors, still going to the same hospitals and other medical providers.

The only difference is, instead of thousands of separately administered programs run with outrageous waste, there would be one health insurance program in America for Members of Congress, for the poorest people in our country, for all of us. In that process, we would save hundreds of billions of dollars in bureaucratic waste. In terms of benefits, what would you get? A single-payer program covers all medically necessary care, including primary care, emergency care, hospital services, mental health services, prescriptions, eye care, dental care, rehabilitation services, and nursing home care as well. In terms of medical decisions, those decisions under a single-payer program would be made by the doctors and the patients, not by bureaucrats in insurance companies.

If we move toward a single-payer program, we could save $350 billion a year in administrative simplification, bulk purchasing, improved access with greater use of preventive services, and earlier diagnosis of illness.

People will be able to get to the doctor when they need to rather than waiting until they are sick and ending up in a hospital.

Further, and importantly, like other countries with a national health care program, we would be able to negotiate drug prices with the pharmaceutical industry, and we would end the absurdity of Americans being forced to pay two, three, five times more for certain drugs than people around the rest of the world.

Every other industrialized country on Earth primarily funds health care from broad-based taxes in the same way we fund the Defense Department, Social Security, and other agencies of government, and that is how we would fund a national health care program.

Let me be specific about how we would pay for this. What this legislation would do is, No. 1, eliminate—underline "eliminate"—all payments to private insurance companies. So people would not be paying premiums to UnitedHealth, WellPoint, Blue Cross Blue Shield, and other private industry companies—not one penny. The reason for that is that private for-profit health insurance companies in this country would no longer exist.

Instead, this legislation would maintain all of the tax revenue that currently flows into public health programs like Medicare, Medicaid, and CHIP, and it would add to that an income tax increase of 2.2 percent and a payroll tax of 8.7 percent. This payroll tax would replace all other employer expenses for employee health care. In other words, employers in this country, from General Motors to a mom-and-pop store in rural America, would no longer be paying one penny toward private insurance revenue. . . .

Let me end by saying this: This country is in the midst of a horrendous health care crisis. We all know that. We can tinker with the system. We can come up with a 2000-page bill which does this, that, and the other thing. But at the end of the day, if we are going to do what virtually every other country on Earth does—provide comprehensive, universal health care in a cost-effective way, one that does not bankrupt our government or bankrupt individuals—if we are going to do that, we are going to have to take on the private insurance companies and tell them very clearly that they are no longer needed. Thanks for your service. We don't need you anymore.

A Medicare-for-all program is the way to go. I know it is not going to pass today. I know we do not have the votes. I know the insurance company and the drug lobbyists will fight us to the death. But, mark my words, Madam President, the day will come when this country will do the right thing. On that day, we will pass a Medicare-for-all single-payer system.

Bernie Facts

- Bernie repeatedly introduced legislation in Congress to enact a single-payer health care system, including the 2013 American Health Security Act.

- Bernie believed that the Affordable Care Act did not go far enough because it guaranteed huge profits to the insurance and drug industries. However, when the Supreme Court upheld the ACA in *King v. Burwell*, Bernie praised the ruling that preserved coverage for millions of people, adding, "A Medicare-for-all, single-payer system would provide better care at less cost for more Americans."

- To highlight the outrageous cost of prescription drugs, Bernie pioneered the tactic of taking busloads of Vermont residents— most of them seniors—to Canada where they could buy cheap pharmaceuticals.

3

Education

End Student Debt,
Make Public-College Tuition Free

Crippling student debt [is] a problem which prevents many from finding meaningful employment, a place to live, or the ability to start a family or business. Even worse though the rapidly rising cost of higher education has made it unaffordable for many families, which is why so many must take on absurd amounts of student loan debt. A democratic country needs an educated populace to survive. In the modern world an educated work force is a necessity when the brightest minds from all around the globe are the competition our students face. Something needs to change and Bernie Sanders has long advocated for that change.

—Students for Bernie Sanders,
studentsforberniesanders.com

Far too many aspiring students are either deterred from pursuing a degree due to exorbitant tuition rates or are saddled with crippling debt upon graduation. That is why Sen. Sanders' new bill that eliminates tuition . . . for all public colleges and universities is so sorely needed.

—Randi Weingarten, president of the
American Federation of Teachers, in response to
Bernie's introduction of the College for All Act

I'm a Republican, but I'll be voting for a Democrat next election if @BernieSanders is their candidate.

—Emily Gosnell, aspiring teacher getting
her master's degree at Azusa Pacific University

Millennials are embracing Bernie because he has clearly pegged student debt as a national crisis and is proposing to make four-year colleges tuition-free. Just consider this number: College debt load has risen to over $1 trillion, according to the Federal Reserve Board of New York.[9]

Of course, voters will ask Bernie: How do you pay for that? Bernie proposes putting a teensy charge on Wall Street transactions, an amount so small that the average investor would not even notice it. But big Wall Street firms will pay a fair share via this financial transactions tax, which could raise up to $300 billion per year. Asking the top one-tenth of 1 percent who work in the financial industry—the very people who depend on an educated workforce to keep the wheels of the financial industry running—to pay to make sure everyone gets a shot at college is a pretty fair deal, as Bernie sees it. —J.T.

Bernie's introduction to the College for All Act, a bill to provide free tuition at four-year public colleges and universities, May 19, 2015[10]

Too many of our young people cannot afford a college education and those who are leaving college are faced with crushing debt. It is a national disgrace that hundreds of thousands of young Americans today do not go to college, not because they are unqualified, but because they cannot afford it.

This is absolutely counter-productive to our efforts to create a strong competitive economy and a vibrant middle class. This disgrace has got to end.

In a global economy, when our young people are competing with workers from around the world, we have got to have the best educated workforce possible. And, that means that we have got to make college affordable. We have got to make sure that every qualified American in this country who wants to go to college can go to college—regardless of income.

Further, it is unacceptable that 40 million Americans are drowning in more than $1.2 trillion in student loan debt.

It is unacceptable that millions of college graduates cannot afford to buy their first home or their first new car because of the high interest rates they are paying on student debt.

It is unacceptable that, in many instances, interest rates on student loans are two to three times higher than on auto loans.

Let's be clear: other nations around the world understand the benefits of having an educated workforce that isn't burdened with enormous student debt. Other countries recognize that allowing all qualified students, regardless of income, to achieve a higher education is an investment in the economic prosperity of their people.

For example:

- Last year, tuition was eliminated in Germany because policymakers believed that charging $1,300 per year was discouraging students from attending college. $1,300 per year, and that tuition was eliminated.
- In Denmark, not only is college free of tuition and fees, people who go to college in that country actually get paid to go to college.
- In Finland, Norway and Sweden, tuition and fees are free not only for their citizens, but in many cases, foreign students as well.
- And, Chile, which has the highest level of income inequality in Latin America, will implement free college tuition next year, and pay for it by increasing taxes on corporations.

But, it's not just other countries around the world that are doing the right thing. There was a time, not so many years ago, when we in the United States understood the importance of making college available to all qualified students, regardless of income.

A generation ago, our nation's public colleges and universities were the pathways for all students, no matter their family background, to enter the middle class.

For example, the University of California system, considered by many to be the crown jewel of public higher education in this country, did not begin charging tuition until the 1980s.

In 1965, average tuition at a four-year public university was just $243, and many of the best colleges—such as the City University of New York—did not charge any tuition.

And this investment in higher education worked—the United States once led the world in the percentage of young Americans with college degrees. Sadly, today, we are in 12th place.

It is time for a fundamental change in how we approach the financing of higher education, and the legislation I will introduce today will do just that.

The College for All Act will provide free tuition at every public college and university in this country.

This means that ANY student, regardless of his or her background or income, who has the ability and desire, will be able to get the education they need and the education they deserve. This legislation opens the door for a middle class life to millions of young Americans and will make our economy stronger and more productive.

This legislation will establish a partnership with states by developing a matching grant program which would provide $2 in federal funding for every dollar that states spend on making tuition-free higher education in public colleges and universities.

This legislation would also expand the federal work study program.

This legislation not only addresses the crisis of college affordability, but it also deals with another issue of huge consequence for millions of families in this country. And, that is the incredibly oppressive burden of crushing student loan debt.

This legislation will allow every American with student debt to refinance their loans, so that borrowers will always be able to take advantage of favorable interest rates. It makes no sense to me that Americans can refinance their homes when interest rates are low, and that somebody can purchase a car at two percent interest rates, but millions of college graduates are stuck with interest rates of 5, 6, 7 percent sometimes for decades. That makes no sense. That is grossly unfair. This bill would cut student loan interest rates in half and lower the rate to about 2 percent for undergraduates.

In addition, this legislation would eliminate the obscene profit that the federal government makes through the student loan program—some $89 billion over a ten year period. The federal government should not be profiting off of student loans provided to low and moderate income families.

The truth is that providing free tuition at public colleges and universities, and reducing the burden of student debt in this country is an expensive proposition.

So how are we going to pay for it?

How are we going to pay for this estimated $750 billion over the next ten years?

And, here's the answer. At a time of massive income and wealth inequality, at a time when trillions of dollars in wealth have left the pockets of the middle class and have gone to the top one-tenth of one percent, at a time when the wealthiest people in this country have made huge amounts of money from risky derivative transactions and the soaring value of the stock market, this legislation would impose a Wall Street speculation fee on Wall Street investment houses and hedge funds.

More than 1,000 economists have endorsed a tax on Wall Street speculation and today some 40 countries throughout the world have imposed a financial transactions tax including Britain, Germany, France, Switzerland, China, India, South Korea, Hong Kong, Singapore, Taiwan and Brazil.

My legislation would impose a Wall Street speculation fee of 0.5 percent on stock trades (that's 50 cents for every $100 worth of stock), a 0.1 percent fee on bonds, and a 0.005 percent fee on derivatives.

It has been estimated that this legislation would raise up to $300 billion a year.

We must revolutionize our nation's higher education system. We must invest in the young people today, because they are our nation's future doctors, teachers, engineers, scientists and senators—so they can ensure our economy and our nation as a whole have an edge in the 21st Century.

Bernie Facts

- In May 2015, Bernie introduced the College for All Act, which would provide free tuition to any public college or university—and showed how he would pay for it.

- Bernie isn't new to the mission of looking out for college-aged people. In 2014, he sponsored a bill to "help students earn college credits in high school in order to cut the cost of earning a college diploma." The bill was endorsed by the American Association of State Colleges and Universities, the American Association of Community Colleges, the National Association of Independent Colleges and Universities, and the National Association for College Admission Counseling.

- Bernie also sees education as critical for younger people and veterans. When the Senate reauthorized the Head Start program in 2007, Bernie made sure the bill expanded eligibility for Head Start by fighting for more funding and making sure the program had the flexibility to use money for Early Head Start (ages birth through three). He also was an original cosponsor and key supporter of the Post-9/11 GI Bill, which authorized the most significant expansion of veterans' education benefits in more than fifty years.

4

Environment

Save the Planet, Transform Our Energy Use

He's been the most consistent and proactive voice in the entire Keystone fight. Everything that's been needed— from speeches on the floor to legislation to demands that the State Department change its absurd review process—he and his staff have done immediately and with a high degree of professionalism. On climate stuff he's been the most aggressive voice in the Senate, rivaled only by Sheldon Whitehouse.

—Bill McKibben, 350.org founder who has led
the fight to stop the Keystone XL pipeline[11]

Bernie is a longtime champion of preserving the environment and battling climate change. He's led the opposition to the Keystone Pipeline. Senator Barbara Boxer (D-CA) called Bernie's proposal for a carbon tax to discourage the use of coal, oil, and other fossil fuels the "the gold standard" of climate change legislation. He has also proposed major investments in clean, renewable energy. On Earth Day this year, Sanders and Rep. Keith Ellison (D-MN) introduced legislation to eliminate tax breaks and other subsidies for the fossil fuels industry. —J.T.

Statement from Bernie's campaign website about climate change[12]

The United States must lead the world in tackling climate change to make certain that this planet is habitable for our children and grandchildren. We must transform our energy system away from polluting fossil fuels and towards energy efficiency and sustainability.

Millions of homes and buildings need to be weatherized, and we need to greatly accelerate technological progress in wind and solar power generation.

Unless we take bold action to address climate change, our children, grandchildren, and great-grandchildren are going to look back on this period in history and ask a very simple question: Where were they? Why didn't the United States of America, the most powerful nation on earth, lead the international community in cutting greenhouse gas emissions and preventing the devastating damage that the scientific community was sure would come?

From an interview with the author, *Playboy*, November 2013

When you talk about hyper-capitalism, you're seeing people at the heads of coal companies and oil companies willing to sacrifice the well-being of the entire planet to their short-term profits. You got the entire scientific community saying that we have got to be very, very aggressive in cutting greenhouse gas emissions. And these folks are funding phony organizations to try to create doubt about the reality of global warming. That is just, you know, quite incredible. They're willing to destroy the planet for short-term profits. And I regard that as just, you know, incomprehensible. Incomprehensible. And because of their power over the political process, you're seeing what amounts to a deafening silence in the United States Congress and in other bodies around the world about the severity of the problem. . . .

You know, we had a 9/11, terrible incident. Three thousand missing people were killed. You have the scientists telling us that global warming will result in incredible drought, flooding, wildfires, the rise of the sea to flood coastal cities resulting in just huge dislocation for millions and millions of people. Not to mention billions and billions of dollars in rebuilding from extreme weather disturbances. Where's the rising up and saying we've got to move aggressively and to address this. Global warming is a far more serious problem than Al-Qaeda is for a second.

From Bernie's Senate floor statement on
January 7, 2015, taken from the *Congressional Record*[13]

I believe that decades from now our kids and our grandchildren will scratch their heads and they will say: What world were these people—Members of Congress—living in in 2015 when they voted for this Keystone Pipeline? How did it happen that they did not listen to the overwhelming majority of scientists who told us we have to cut greenhouse gas emissions, not increase them? I think our kids and our grandchildren will be saying to us: Why did you do that to us? Why did you leave this planet less habitable than it could have been? ...

Climate change is one of the great threats not only facing our country but facing the entire planet. It has the capability of causing severe harm to our economy, to our food supply, to access to water, and it raises all kinds of international national security issues. ...

Scientists are not the only people warning us about the danger of climate change. Hear what the Department of Defense has to say about the impact of climate change on international and national security. What they point out—and I think what every sensible person understands—is that when people are unable to grow the food they need because of drought, when flood destroys their homes, when people throughout the world are forced to struggle for limited natural resources in order to survive, this lays the groundwork for the migration of people and international conflict. That is what the Department of Defense tells us.

Now, given all of the scientific evidence and given the concerns raised by our own Department of Defense and national security experts all over the world and given the fact that the most recent decade—the last 10 years—was the Nation's warmest on record, one would think that when the National Climate Assessment warns us that global warming could exceed 10 degrees Fahrenheit in the United States by the end of the century—can we imagine this planet becoming 10 degrees Fahrenheit warmer and what this means to the planet? When sea levels have already risen by nearly 7 inches over the last century and are expected to rise another 10 inches to 2.6 feet by the end of the century—when all of that is on the table, one would think this Senate would be saying: All right, we have an international crisis. How do we reverse climate change? Instead, what the debate is about is how we transport some of the dirtiest oil in the world and thereby cause more carbon emissions into the atmosphere.

I suspect our kids and our grandchildren will look back on this period and say: What world were you living in? Why did you do that to us?

It would seem to me that what we should be debating here is how we impose a tax on carbon so that we can break our dependence on fossil fuel. That is what we should be discussing, not how we increase carbon emissions. We should be discussing what kind of legislation we bring forward that moves us aggressively toward energy efficiency, weatherization, and such sustainable energies as wind, solar, and geothermal. That is the kind of bill that should be on the floor. We should be having a debate about legislation that makes our transportation system far more efficient, that expands rail and helps us get cars and trucks off the road. We should be having a debate about how we can create the kind of automobiles that run on electricity and make them less expensive and how we can get cars running 80 to 100 miles per gallon. Those are the kinds of debates and that is the kind of legislation we should be having on the floor, not how do we expand the production and the transportation of some of the dirtiest oil on the planet.

In my view, the U.S. Congress in a very profound way should not be in the business of rejecting science because when we reject science, we become the laughingstock of the world. How do we go forward? How do we prepare legislation if it is not based on scientific evidence? And to say to the overwhelming majority of scientists that we are ignoring what they are telling us and we are going to move in exactly the wrong direction I think makes us look like fools in front of the entire world. How do we go forward and tell China and India and Russia and countries around the world that climate change is a huge planetary crisis at the same time as we are facilitating the construction of the Keystone Pipeline? . . .

Our job now is not to bring more carbon into the atmosphere; it is to transform our energy system away from coal, away from oil, away from fossil fuel, and toward energy efficiency and sustainable energy. That should be the direction of this country, and we should lead the world in moving in that direction.

Bernie Facts

- In 2013, Bernie introduced the Climate Protection Act. Cosponsored by Senator Barbara Boxer (D-CA), the act would make a large investment in alternative energies and energy-efficiency measures, as well as taxing carbon and methane emissions.[14]

- In 2013, Bernie introduced the Residential Energy Savings Act, which would fund programs that assist residents in retrofitting their homes to upgrade energy efficiency. He also introduced the Sustainable Energy Act, which would eliminate billions of dollars in tax subsidies to the oil, natural gas, and coal industries.

- In 2010, Bernie introduced the 10 Million Solar Roofs & 10 Million Gallons of Solar Hot Water Act to boost the development of solar power in the United States.

5

Taxes

The Wealthy Need to Pay Their Fair Share

When people like us are working sixty hours a week, and can still barely afford to survive, but people like the Waltons are getting tax breaks of more money than I will see in my lifetime, there is something wrong.

—Levy Morrow, Colorado resident, at Sanders rally in Denver[15]

Bernie has opposed the bad tax deals—made by corporate lobbyist-funded political parties no matter which party controlled Congress or the White House—that give more tax breaks to corporations and to the richest 1 percent while placing a greater burden on everyone else. In 2010, Bernie's strong opposition to the extension of the Bush tax cuts—which would bring deep cuts in Medicaid, food stamps, and other health and safety-net programs—motivated him to take to the floor of the Senate for more than eight hours denouncing a bipartisan proposal to give more money to the wealthiest people in the country. The marathon speech was an immediate social media hit and a historic civics lesson for every C-SPAN viewer as Bernie charted the divide between rich and poor.   —J.T.

From Bernie's marathon Senate floor speech, December 10, 2010[16]

Last year, ExxonMobil had, for them, a very bad year. They only made $19 billion in profit. Based on $19 billion, you might be surprised to know ExxonMobil not only paid nothing in taxes, they got a $156 million return from the IRS. How is that? For those of you who are working in an office, working in a factory, earning your $30,000, $40,000, $50,000, $60,000 a year, you pay taxes.

But if you are ExxonMobil, and you made $19 billion in profits last year, not only did you not pay any taxes this year, you got $156 million in return.

Furthermore, according to a report from Citizens for Tax Justice, 82 Fortune 500 companies in America, paid zero or less in Federal income taxes in at least 1 year from 2001 to 2003. The Citizens for Tax Justice report goes on to say:

> In the years they paid no income tax, these companies earned $102 billion in U.S. profits. But instead of paying $35.6 billion in income taxes, as the statutory 35 percent corporate tax rate seems to require, these companies generated so many excess tax breaks that they received outright tax rebate checks from the U.S. Treasury totaling $12.6 billion.

If you are a large corporation and you have a good lawyer or a good accountant, you know what to do. You invest your money in the Cayman Islands and in Bermuda, and you don't have to pay American taxes.

I do not want to see my kids and grandchildren pay more in taxes because we have borrowed money from China to increase the national debt in order to give tax breaks to millionaires and billionaires who have done extraordinarily well in recent years and, by the way, have seen a significant decline in their effective tax rate.

Press statement, June 25, 2015, upon introducing his proposal to raise the estate tax on a few hundred of the wealthiest families in the country[17]

Next week we will be celebrating the 4th of July—the day when the founders of our country declared independence from what they viewed as a tyrannical aristocracy in England.

Yet today, in many respects, the tyrannical aristocracy is no longer a foreign power, but a billionaire class which now has unprecedented economic and political power over the American people. In fact, if we do not make the necessary changes to reduce skyrocketing wealth and income inequality, this country is well on its way towards becoming an oligarchy—a nation owned and controlled by a handful of extraordinarily wealthy and powerful people.

Let's be clear: The United States is the wealthiest nation in the history of the world, but the vast majority of the American people don't sense that, don't feel that, because almost all of the wealth is concentrated in the hands of a tiny few.

In the year 2015, the U.S. has by far the most unequal distribution of wealth and income of any major developed country on earth, and this inequality is worse than at any time in our country's history since 1928.

The fact of the matter is that, over the past 40 years, we have witnessed an enormous transfer of wealth from the middle class and working families to multi-millionaires and billionaires.

According to the most recent statistics, the share of the nation's wealth going to the bottom 90 percent of Americans has gone down from 36 percent in 1985 to just 22.8 percent in 2013. Meanwhile, over that same time period, the top one-tenth of one percent saw its share of the nation's wealth more than double going from 10 percent in 1985 to 22 percent today. In other words, the top one-tenth of one percent own nearly as much wealth as the bottom 90 percent of Americans.

In the last two years, the wealthiest 15 people in this country increased their wealth by more than $170 billion. That increase in wealth is more than what is owned by the bottom 130 million Americans combined. Meanwhile, the typical family in 2013 had substantially less wealth than it did a decade ago.

Today, the richest family in this country—the Walton family of Walmart—is now worth more than the bottom 42 percent of the American people.

In terms of income, the top one percent earns more than the bottom 50 percent. Since the Great Recession of 2008, 99 percent of all income gains in the U.S. have gone to the top one percent. Meanwhile, while the rich have become even richer, the percentage of senior citizens living in poverty has gone up and we have the highest rate of childhood poverty of any major advanced country on Earth.

Now, at a time when the rich are getting richer, and when almost all new income and wealth is going to the people on top, how have my Republican colleagues responded to this grotesque level of inequality? Well, what they have done unbelievably is to pass legislation which provides a $269 billion tax break to the wealthiest 5,400 Americans in this country—the top two-tenths of 1 percent—by repealing the estate tax. In other words, the Republicans address income and wealth inequality by giving a gigantic tax break to the wealthiest of the wealthy.

This is wrong morally. We should not exacerbate income and wealth inequality. It is wrong economically. We need to be putting more money into the hands of working families, not the very rich. Instead of repealing this tax, which makes the very rich even richer, we need to substantially increase the estate tax to make sure that the wealthiest Americans in this country pay their fair share.

That is not just what Bernie Sanders believes. More than a century ago, President Teddy Roosevelt, a good Republican, fought for the creation of a progressive estate tax in order to reduce the enormous concentration of wealth that existed during the Gilded Age.

As Teddy Roosevelt said, "The absence of effective state, and, especially, national restraint upon unfair money-getting has tended to create a small class of enormously wealthy and economically powerful men, whose chief object is to hold and increase their power. The prime need is to change the conditions which enable these men to accumulate power . . . Therefore, I believe in a . . . graduated inheritance tax on big fortunes, properly safeguarded against evasion and increasing rapidly in amount with the size of the estate."

While Roosevelt spoke those words on August 31, 1910, they are even more relevant today. Income and wealth inequality is the great moral issue of our time. It is the great economic issue of our time, and, as a result of *Citizens United*, it is the great political issue of our time. No great nation will flourish when so few have so much and so many have so little.

One of the most straightforward ways to address wealth inequality, invest in the disappearing middle class, and preserve our democracy is to enact a progressive estate tax on multi-millionaires and billionaires. As you know, for almost a hundred years, this country has had an estate tax on the books that only taxes the inheritances of the very wealthiest people in this country. Today, that tax only applies to the wealthiest two-tenths of one percent—and my Republican colleagues, who are so anxious to protect the interests of the wealthy and powerful, want to eliminate that. But I think we should move in a very different direction. And that is why I am introducing the Responsible Estate Tax Act. This legislation, which only applies to the top three-tenths of one percent, includes a progressive estate tax structure so that the super wealthy pay more.

Bernie Facts

- When he was in the House, Bernie voted against the Economic Growth and Tax Relief Reconciliation Act, which authorized the Bush tax cuts for the wealthy in 2001. He also voted against the second round of Bush tax cuts for the wealthy in 2003.

- In 2010, Bernie again fought the extension of Bush tax cuts that favor the top 5 percent and will cost the nation $3.2 trillion between 2001 and 2021. Those tax reductions will put a heavier burden on regular working people and result in deep cuts in important social programs.

- Bernie proposed legislation in June 2015, to increase estate tax rates on the top three-tenths of 1 percent of Americans, those who inherit more than $3.5 million. The bill would also create a new billionaire surtax of 10 percent, which would impact only 530 billionaires who are worth a combined $2.6 trillion; end loopholes allowing billionaire families to set up dynasty trusts to avoid taxes; and close loopholes used by the wealthy to avoid estate taxes.

6

Wall Street

Too Big to Fail? Too Big to Exist

*I haven't seen anybody prosecuted and joining Bernie Mad-
off in jail as a cell mate.*

—Francisco Ramos, forty-seven,
Florida land surveyor[18]

For many years—before it became popular—Sanders has been one
of the leading critics of Wall Street and the big banks. He supports
breaking up the big banks so they are no longer able to play such
a major role in economic decisions. He also is pushing a bill for a
financial transactions tax—a tiny surcharge on the sale of stocks,
bonds, derivatives, Treasury securities, and other financial instruments traded daily in vast quantities. Such a surcharge could, by
various estimates, raise between $50 and $350 billion per year in
a way that for most taxpayers would be painless and would help
underwrite Bernie's proposal to make a four-year college degree
free. He has supported previous financial transaction tax efforts
going back to 2013, when he got behind legislation introduced
by then senator Tom Harkin (D-IA) and Representative Peter
DeFazio (D-OR). —J.T.

From Bernie's marathon
Senate floor speech, December 10, 2010[19]

I think what is most surprising for the American people is not just
the bailout of Wall Street and the financial institutions, and the
bailout of large American corporations such as General Electric,
but I think the American people would find it very strange that
at a time when the American automobile sector was on the verge

of collapse, the Federal Reserve was also bailing out Toyota and Mitsubishi, two Japanese carmakers, by purchasing nearly $5 billion worth of their commercial paper from November 5, 2008, through January 30, 2009.

While virtually no American-made cars or products of any kind are bought in Japan, I think the American people would be shocked to learn that the Fed extended over $380 billion to the Central Bank of Japan to bail out banks in that country.

Furthermore, I think the American people are interested to know that the Fed bailed out the Korea Development Bank, the wholly owned, state-owned Bank of South Korea, by purchasing over $2 billion of its commercial paper. The sole purpose of the Korea Development Bank is to finance and manage major industrial projects to enhance the national economy not of the United States of America but of South Korea. I am not against South Korea. I wish the South Koreans all the luck in the world. But it should not be the taxpayers of the United States lending their banks' money to create jobs in South Korea. I would suggest maybe we want to create jobs in the United States of America. At the same time, the Fed also extended over $40 billion for the Central Bank of South Korea so that it had enough money to bail out its own banks.

What we saw is people on Wall Street operating from a business model based on fraud, based on dishonesty, understanding that the likelihood of them ever getting caught was small, that if things got very bad, they would be bailed out by the taxpayers, understanding that they are too powerful to ever be put in jail, to be indicted, understanding that in this country when you are a CEO on Wall Street, you have so much wealth and so much power and so many lawyers and so many friends in Congress, you could do pretty much anything you want and not much is going to happen to you—and they did it. Their greed and recklessness and their illegal behavior destroyed this economy.

What they did to the American people is so horrible. Here we had a middle class which was already being battered as a result of trade agreements, loss of manufacturing jobs, health care costs going up, couldn't afford to send their children to college—that had gone on for years—and then these guys started pushing worthless and complicated financial instruments and the whole thing explodes.

Today, after we bailed out all these large banks, three out of four of them are now much larger than they were before. Today, Bank of America, JPMorgan Chase, Citigroup, and Wells Fargo—the four largest financial institutions in this country—hold about $7.4 trillion in assets, and that is equal to over half the Nation's estimated total output last year. Four financial institutions have assets worth more than 52 percent of our total output last year.

Instead of breaking up these folks, these large institutions, we let them get bigger. The four largest banks in America now issue one out of every two mortgages, two out of three credit cards, and hold $4 out of every $10 in bank deposits in the entire country.

If any of these financial institutions were to get into major trouble again, taxpayers would be on the hook for another substantial bailout. **We cannot allow that to happen** [emphasis added].

From Bernie's introduction to the Too Big to Fail, Too Big to Exist Act, May 6, 2015

In the midst of this grotesque level of income and wealth inequality is Wall Street.

As we all know, the greed, recklessness, and illegal behavior on Wall Street drove this country into the worst recession since the Great Depression. Millions of Americans lost their jobs, homes, life savings, and ability to send their kids to college.

The middle class is still suffering from the horrendous damage huge financial institutions and insurance companies did to this country in 2008.

Now, I voted for Dodd-Frank, but let's not kid ourselves. Dodd-Frank was a very modest piece of legislation. Dodd-Frank did not end much of the casino-style gambling on Wall Street.

In fact, much of this reckless activity is still going on today.

It seems like almost every day we read about one giant financial institution after another being fined or reaching settlements for their reckless, unfair, and deceptive activities.

In fact, since 2009, huge financial institutions have paid $176 billion in fines and settlement payments for fraudulent and unscrupulous activities.

Bank of America alone has paid $57.9 billion, JPMorgan has paid 31.4 billion, and Citigroup has paid $12.8 billion in fines and settlements.

Bank of America has been fined for foreclosure abuses, selling toxic mortgage-backed securities, LIBOR manipulation, and currency rigging.

It should make every American very nervous that in this weak regulatory environment, the financial supervisors in this country and around the world are still able to uncover an enormous amount of fraud on Wall Street to this day.

I fear very much that the financial system is even more fragile than many people may perceive.

This huge issue cannot be swept under the rug.

It has got to be addressed. . . .

No single financial institution should be so large that its failure would cause catastrophic risk to millions of Americans or to our nation's economic well-being.

No single financial institution should have holdings so extensive that its failure would send the world economy into crisis.

If an institution is too big to fail, it is too big to exist and that is the bottom line.

And, let's be clear: the reason we are here today is not just because of the danger these institutions pose to taxpayers.

The enormous concentration of ownership within the financial sector is hurting the middle class and damaging the economy by limiting choices and raising prices for consumers and small businesses.

Today, just six huge financial institutions have assets of nearly $10 trillion which is equal to nearly 60 percent of GDP. These huge banks handle more than two-thirds of all credit card purchases, write over 35 percent of the mortgages, and control nearly half of all bank deposits in this country.

If the American people are wondering why tens of millions of Americans are being charged interest rates of more than 20 percent on their credit cards, while big banks can receive virtually zero interest loans from the Federal Reserve, the lack of competition in the banking industry is a major reason for that.

If Teddy Roosevelt were alive today, do you know what he would say?

He would say break 'em up. And he would be right.

And that's exactly why we are here today.

The bill that I am introducing today with Congressman Brad Sherman would require regulators at the Financial Stability Oversight Council to establish "Too Big To Fail" list of financial institutions and other huge entities whose failure would pose a catastrophic risk on the United States economy without a taxpayer bailout.

This list must include, but is not limited to: JPMorgan Chase, Bank of America, Citigroup, Goldman Sachs, Wells Fargo, and Morgan Stanley.

All of these financial institutions have already been deemed "systemically important banks" by the Financial Stability Board, the G20 body that monitors and makes recommendations about the global financial system.

Within a year, the Treasury Secretary would be required to break up financial institutions on this list so that they cannot cause another financial crisis ever again.

Importantly, under this bill, none of the institutions on the "Too Big to Fail list" would be able to receive a taxpayer bailout from the Federal Reserve; nor could they gamble with the federally insured bank deposits of the American people while they are on this list. . . .

The function of banking should not be about making as much profits as possible gambling on derivatives and other esoteric financial instruments.

The function of banking should be to provide affordable loans to small businesses to create jobs in the productive economy.

The function of banking should be to provide affordable loans to Americans to purchase homes and cars.

Wall Street cannot be an island onto itself.

The position I hold today is not something new for me.

In 1994, I cast the only no vote in the House Financial Services Committee against legislation that allowed large out-of-state banks to acquire locally owned community banks. . . .

In 1999, I helped lead the opposition against repealing the Glass-Steagall Act that allowed commercial banks, insurance companies, and investment banks to merge, and I was one of the leading opponents of the efforts of Alan Greenspan, Robert Rubin, and Lawrence Summers [who] all told us how wonderful it would be if we deregulated Wall Street back in the '90s.

Now, I know that passing this bill will not be easy.

The fact of the matter is that Congress does not regulate Wall Street; Wall Street regulates Congress.

But the time has come to say enough is enough!

The time has come to truly end too big to fail!

Bernie Facts

- Bernie led the charge for the first-ever top-to-bottom audit of the Federal Reserve Board that found the Fed had made $16 trillion in secret loans to bail out American and foreign banks and businesses during the recent financial crisis.

- Bernie introduced the Too Big to Fail, Too Big to Exist Act in May 2015, to break up the largest banks so that the people would not be on the hook for the cost of bailing out one or more of those banks to avoid economic chaos. Bernie was not new to such efforts: In 2009, with the banking crisis in full swing, he introduced a similar bill (also titled the Too Big to Fail, Too Big to Exist Act) and then, determined to push the issue, reintroduced the bill in 2013.

- Bernie has introduced a financial transaction tax, which would enact a small fee on Wall Street transactions. It is similar to efforts he supported in the past.

7

Workers

Unions and Rebuilding the Middle Class

Senator Bernie Sanders gets it; the attack on unions is an attack on workers and the middle class. We are all in this together.

—Tumblr message, New York State AFL-CIO, July 2, 2014[20]

Bernie has been always a stalwart ally and defender of the rights of workers to join a union. He regularly draws a direct connection between the economic crisis facing all Americans on the one hand, and the attacks against unions on the other hand.

Soon after he joined the Senate, he gave a floor speech in support of Senator Ted Kennedy's (D-MA) bill to enact the Employee Free Choice Act, which was the top priority of organized labor because it would strengthen the democratic rights of workers to join a union. —J.T.

Bernie's Senate floor statement supporting the Employee Free Choice Act, June 25, 2007[21]

Year after year, millions of American workers have been working longer hours for lower wages. In Vermont, it is not uncommon for people to work two jobs and on occasion work three jobs in order to cobble together an income in order to cobble together some health insurance.

Consider the facts: Since 2001, median household income has fallen by nearly $1,300; wages and salaries now make up their lowest share of the economy in nearly six decades; the number of Americans who lack health insurance has grown by 6.8 million since 2001, to over 46 million Americans without any health insurance today; the number of Fortune 1,000 companies that have frozen or terminated their pension plans has more than tripled since 2001.

Indeed, the middle class itself has shrunk. Over 5 million more Americans have slipped into poverty since the year 2000. So what we are seeing is the average American worker working longer hours for lower wages.

Today there are millions of Americans who work who scarcely have any vacation time whatsoever. People are losing their health insurance, they are losing their pensions, and they are sitting around looking at the reality that if we do not turn this around, their kids will be even worse off than they are all at the same time technology is exploding and worker productivity is increasing.

Meanwhile, while the middle class shrinks and poverty increases, corporate profits today make up their largest share of the economy since the 1960s. While the middle class is shrinking, millionaires and billionaires in this country have never had it so good since the late 1920s.

Today, the wealthiest 1 percent of Americans own more wealth than the bottom 90 percent. The CEOs of our largest corporations now earn 400 times as much as the average worker. This is not just an economic issue, this is a moral issue. Is this what America is supposed to be about, the wealthiest 1 percent owning more wealth than the bottom 90 percent, and the gap between the rich and the poor growing wider every day, as the middle class continues to shrink. I do not believe that is what America is supposed to be.

At the same time, workers are seeing a decline in real wages, are being forced to pay more for their health insurance, and are seeing their pensions slashed. The CEOs of large corporations are making out like bandits. Just one simple example: Several years ago, the former CEO of ExxonMobil, Lee Raymond, received a $400 million retirement package—while we are paying over $3 for a gallon of gas, and ExxonMobil, last year, enjoyed the highest profits of any corporation in the history of the world. . . .

And on and on it goes, CEOs making out like bandits, workers paying $3 for a gallon of gas, losing their health insurance, losing their pensions, losing their homes. . . .

There are a lot of reasons for the growing inequality in our economy, and economists may differ, but there is clearly agreement on some of the basic reasons the gap between the rich and the poor is growing wider and the middle class is shrinking. The failure, up until very recently, to raise the minimum wage is an obvious example. Millions and millions and millions of workers today—before the new minimum wage goes into effect—are making $5.15 an hour. Yes, the U.S. Congress has provided hundreds of billions of dollars in tax breaks for the wealthiest 1 percent, but we could not raise the minimum wage until a few weeks ago. . . .

But perhaps the most significant reason for the decline in the middle class is [that] the rights of workers to join together and bargain for better wages, better benefits, and better working conditions have been severely undermined over the years.

Today, if an employee is engaged in a union organizing campaign, that employee has a one in five chance of getting fired.

Today, half of all employers threaten to close or relocate their business if workers choose to form a union.

Today, when workers become interested in forming unions, 92 percent of private sector employers force employees to attend closed-door meetings to hear antiunion propaganda; 80 percent require supervisors to attend training sessions on attacking unions; 78 percent require supervisors to deliver antiunion messages to workers they oversee; and 75 percent hire outside consultants to run antiunion campaigns.

In 2005 alone, over 30,000 workers were discriminated against, losing wages or even their jobs, for exercising their constitutional right of freedom of association—a right guaranteed under the Constitution of the United States.

Further, Human Rights Watch has said: *Freedom of association is a right under severe, often buckling pressure when workers in the United States try to exercise it.*

The right to come together to form a union is a constitutional right. It is under severe, unprecedented attack today.

Even when workers—who are faced with all of these enormous obstacles—win union elections, more than one-third of the victories do not result in a first contract for workers.

Today, corporate executives are routinely negotiating obscenely high compensation packages for themselves, but then they deny their own employees their ability to come together to create better wages and working conditions and better lives for themselves.

That is wrong.

This Senate has to stand up for those workers.

It is time to turn this around. It is time to stand up for the working people of this country. That is what the Employee Free Choice Act is all about. . . .

This legislation is very simple. The Employee Free Choice Act would simply allow workers to join unions when a majority sign valid authorization cards stating they want a union as their bargaining representative. As Senator Kennedy has correctly pointed out, card check recognition was the law of the land in the United States from 1941 to 1966. In other words, all this legislation does is give workers the same rights they had 41 years ago.

More than half of the U.S. workforce—nearly 60 million workers—say they would join a union right now if they had the opportunity. Yet only 12 percent of the workforce has a union.

This is much different from other industrialized countries around the world. In Canada, where card check is the law of the land, twice as many workers belong to unions [as] in the United States. In Britain, where card check recognition is the law of the land, 60 percent of workers belong to unions.

What has strong union participation meant for workers in other countries? This is an important point to be made because it is terribly important we in the Senate see what is going on in the rest of the industrialized world, see and note the benefits workers around the world are receiving that our workers are not.

Just a few examples. In Finland, where two-thirds of workers belong to unions—guess what—unlike college graduates in the United States who are graduating $20,000 in debt, Finland provides a free college education, including law and medical schools, to all qualified citizens. That is pretty good. They encourage young people to go to college and graduate school tuition free.

While the cost of childcare in the United States is skyrocketing—millions of American families cannot afford quality childcare—in Finland, day care is free to all citizens. Unlike the United States, where the 2-week vacation is becoming a thing of the past, in Finland, workers are guaranteed 30 days of paid vacation and 60 days of paid sick leave.

In Norway, where the union participation rate is about 60 percent, women receive 42 weeks of maternal leave at full pay—full pay—while U.S. workers only receive 12 weeks of unpaid maternal leave.

In Belgium, France, and Sweden over 90 percent of workers belong to unions. Workers in those countries all have much stronger pensions, health care, childcare, and vacation benefits than American workers.

In addition to the card check provision, the Employee Free Choice Act would also stiffen penalties against employers who illegally fire or discriminate against workers for their union activity during an organizing or first contract drive.

Perhaps most importantly, this legislation will make it easier for workers who win union elections to negotiate a first contract. We will end the situation where, when workers decide to form a union—they go to negotiate—the employer simply refuses to negotiate.

In order to strengthen America's middle class, we have to restore workers' rights to bargain for better wages, benefits, and working conditions.

After all, union workers in this country earn 30 percent more, on average, than nonunion workers who are performing the same jobs.

Madam President, 80 percent of union workers have employer-provided health insurance; only 49 percent of nonunion workers do.

Madam President, 68 percent of union workers have a guaranteed pension through a defined benefit plan; only 14 percent of nonunion workers do.

Madam President, 62 percent of union workers have short-term disability benefits; only 35 percent of nonunion workers do.

Union workers have, on average, 15 days of paid vacation; while nonunion workers, on average, have fewer than 11 days of paid vacation....

We have to do everything we can from a moral perspective to reverse the decline of the middle class, to lower our poverty rates, to improve the standard of living of American workers, and passing the Employee Free Choice Act is an important step in that direction.

Bernie Facts

- Bernie has supported unions in every fight in Congress, from the attempt in 1995 to ban permanent striker replacements when he was in the House to opposing NAFTA and similar anti-worker trade bills.

- Bernie was a strong supporter of the Employee Free Choice Act, which would strengthen the rights of workers to choose a union without fear of retaliation from employers.

- Bernie has walked picket lines with strikers and acted as an advocate for workers trying to get a better deal, from blue- and white-collar telecommunications workers to tomato workers laboring in slave-like conditions.

8

Family Values
Our Shared Responsibility

Paid leave for parents to stay home with a newborn has been made into a privilege when it should be a basic right. We need comprehensive policy reform to address how we as a nation care for our families. Everyone has the right to experience the bliss of staying home and being fully present for those first months. It's an issue of fairness.

—Lora Smith, mother, Greensboro, North Carolina[22]

Bernie has been one of the strongest advocates for workers' rights to paid leave and vacation. Dating back to his service in the House, he was an unwavering voice for the Family and Medical Leave Act. At the same time, he does not hesitate to point out that, compared with other countries around the world, the United States lags in many aspects of paid leave and vacation, as well as support for women in the workplace.

He recently posed the issue of paid leave and vacation as a rousing call for the nation to embrace a set of true "family values."   —J.T.

Statement released by Bernie's Senate office about the issue of "family values," June 11, 2015[23]

When a mother has a baby and is unable to spend time with that child during the first weeks and months of that baby's life, and is forced back to work because of a lack of money, that is not a family value. That is an attack on everything that a family is supposed to stand for.

When a wife is diagnosed with cancer and a husband cannot get time off of work to take care of her, that is not a family value. That is an attack on everything that a family is supposed to stand for.

When a mother is forced to send her sick child to school because she cannot afford to stay home with her that is not a family value. That is an attack on everything that a family is supposed to stand for.

When a husband, wife, and kids, during the course of an entire year, are unable to spend any time together on vacation—that is not a family value. That is an attack on everything that a family is supposed to stand for.

Let's be clear: in terms of protecting the needs of our families, in terms of real family values, in many respects the United States lags behind virtually every major country on earth.

When you look at what other wealthy countries are doing, what you find is that the United States of America is the only advanced economy that does not guarantee its workers some form of paid family leave, paid sick time or paid vacation time.

In other words, when it comes to basic workplace protections and family benefits, workers in every other major industrialized country in the world get a better deal than workers in the United States.

That is wrong.

That is a travesty.

And that has got to change.

Last place is no place for America.

It is time to join the rest of the industrialized world by showing the people of this country that we are not just a nation that talks about family values but that we are a nation that is prepared to live up to these ideals by making sure that workers in this country have access to paid family leave, paid sick time and paid vacations just like workers in every other wealthy country on earth.

Simply stated it is an outrage that millions of women in this country give birth and then are forced back to work because they don't have the income to stay home with their newborn babies. Virtually every psychologist who has studied this issue understands that the first weeks and months of life are enormously important in terms of the emotional and intellectual development of that person.

And what is most important is the need for mothers and fathers to bond with the baby they have brought to life.

What kind of family value is it when you tell a woman who has just had a baby that she can't spend time with that child, but that she has to go back to work?

That is not a family value.

That is an insult to every mother, father and baby in this country and that has got to change.

The reality is that the Family and Medical Leave Act (FMLA) that was signed into law in 1993 is totally inadequate. Today, nearly 8 out of 10 workers in this country who are eligible to take time off under this law cannot do so because they could not afford it (according to the Department of Labor). Even worse, 40 percent of American workers are not even eligible to receive this unpaid leave because they work for a company with fewer than 50 employees.

In my view, every worker in America should be guaranteed at least 12 weeks of paid family and medical leave—and that is why I am supporting—the FAMILY Act . . . The FAMILY Act would guarantee employees 12 weeks of paid family and medical leave to take care of a baby; to help a family member who is diagnosed with cancer or has some other serious medical condition; or to take care of themselves if they become seriously ill.

And just like Social Security retirement and disability, it is an insurance program that workers would pay into, at a price of about one cup of coffee a week.

But that's not all.

We have also got to make sure that workers in this country have paid sick time.

In my view, it is absurd that low-wage workers in McDonald's who get sick are forced to work because they cannot afford to miss work.

Not only is this bad for the workers who are sick, it is also a public health issue. That is why I am supporting the Healthy Families Act . . . which guarantees seven days of paid sick leave to American workers.

This bill would benefit 43 million Americans who don't already have access to paid sick leave, and it would create a permanent floor in workplaces where employers already provide some paid sick leave. . . .

One hundred years ago workers in this country took to the streets demanding a 40 hour work week. And here we are 100 years later, living in the most technologically advanced economy in human history, and we still don't have [a] 40-hour workweek!

In fact, 85% of working men and 66% of working women are working more than 40 hours a week. What we have are millions of people, working incredible hours—some with two or three jobs—just trying to care for themselves and their families.

Americans now work, by far, the longest hours of any major country on earth—137 hours a year more hours than workers in Japan, 260 hours more than the British and 499 hours more than French workers.

That is why I am introducing legislation today to require employers to provide at least 10 days of paid vacation to workers in this country.

There is no reason that American workers should be denied a benefit that workers in every other advanced economy already enjoy. Again, when you compare the United States to other rich countries in Europe, Australia, Canada, Japan, New Zealand, you discover that we are the only one in the group that doesn't require employers to provide at least 10 days of paid vacation time.

We are every bit as prosperous as they are, and the reason we are so prosperous is because the men and women of this country work so hard. I am not asking for the most generous vacation policy in the world—nothing like what they get in France, Austria or Belgium—but I am going to push for a standard befitting a great nation that takes seriously its commitment to Family Values.

For Bernie, there are other legislative efforts that fall under the broader issue of family values, such as respecting women, supporting a woman's right to control her body and her health care, supporting gender pay equity, and championing the rights of LGBTQ members of society. In the House, he voted in 1996 against the so-called Defense of Marriage Act, which barred federal recognition of gay marriages and was signed by President Bill Clinton. In Vermont, Sanders supported the state's 2000 civil unions law and the 2009 law legalizing gay marriage.   —J.T.

—On LGBTQ Rights—

From an interview with the
Washington Blade, May 15, 2015 [24]

In the United States, I think we have seen in the last 20 to 25 years, some very positive changes in terms of becoming a less discriminatory society. I talk a whole lot about economics, in fact, in terms of economics, we are becoming clearly a nation with more and more wealth inequality. We're losing that battle. But in areas of civil rights, in areas of gay rights, in areas of women's rights, we've made some good progress. . . . We are trying to create a non-discriminatory society where we judge people based on their character, on their abilities, not on the color of their skin, their sexual orientation, their gender. Clearly, as a nation we've made good progress, we have a lot further to go. . . . But where it's also important is that whether you are gay or straight or transgender, you don't have a job, or if you don't have the kind of income you need to live with dignity, you're going to suffer. So, I think what we have to do as a nation is make sure that the jobs we create pay a living wage, which means raising minimum wage, passing pay equity, creating trade policies that work for American workers, expanding Social Security. Those impact every person in American regardless of their sexual orientation.

—On Women's Rights—

From Bernie's speech at the United Against the War on
Women event in Montpelier, Vermont, April 28, 2012 [25]

In the last fifty years, as the result of an enormous amount of effort on the part of the women's movement and their male allies, we as a nation have made significant progress in the fight for gender equality. Clearly, much, much more needs to be done but few would deny that our country has come a very long way in this struggle.

And the message of today, here in Vermont and across the country, is that we are not going back. Not only are we not going to retreat on women's rights, we are going to expand them. We are going forward, not backwards.

We are not returning to the days of back room abortions, when countless women died or were maimed. The decision about abortion must remain a decision for the woman, her family and physician to make, not the government.

We are not going back to the days when women could not have full access to birth control. . . .

We are not going back to the days of wide-scale domestic violence, even if 31 Republican men in the Senate recently voted against the reauthorization of the Violence Against Women Act because it expanded coverage to the gay community and Native Americans.

We are not going back to the days when it was legal for women to be paid less for doing the same work as men. . . .

[W]e must continue and expand our efforts to be national leaders in the fight for gender equality. I have seven beautiful grandchildren, four of whom are girls. Let us all work together in making sure that those four girls, and every girl in our state and country, [have] the same opportunity as anyone else to fulfill their dreams and live their lives without gender discrimination of any kind.

Bernie Facts

- Bernie has cosponsored the Healthy Families Act, which guarantees seven paid sick leave days to every worker.

- Bernie also saw a simple family values idea when he pushed for a doubling of the Low Income Home Energy Assistance Program in 2008, a time when home-heating bills were soaring. The proposal passed overwhelmingly (as part of a larger bill), ensuring that millions of Americans wouldn't go cold in the winter by providing them with financial assistance to pay their heating bills.

- Bernie has supported passing broad leave and vacation benefits since his years in the House in the 1990s, including his strong voice of support for the Family and Medical Leave Act in 1993, which began to set a floor for needed family benefits.

- Bernie has always been a strong supporter of equal rights for the LGBTQ community, dating back to his service as mayor of Burlington.

- Bernie has supported the Paycheck Fairness Act and has been a vocal supporter of women's rights in Congress. In 1996, during a campaign stop in support of Sanders, Gloria Steinem named him an "honorary woman."

9

Society

Expand Social Security, Medicare, and Medicaid

Social Security is also the country's most important anti-poverty program for the nation's children.

—Center for Economic and Policy Research[26]

Bernie has been a relentless defender of Social Security, Medicare, and Medicaid, calling Social Security "the most successful federal program in modern American history" because it has dramatically reduced poverty among senior citizens and other people dependent on the program, including children. Before Social Security was enacted eighty years ago, roughly half of the senior citizens in the United States lived in poverty. Today that number is less than 10 percent.

Bernie has fought attempts by both parties to "reform" programs that are a lifeline for millions of Americans. He is the founder of the Senate Defending Social Security Caucus and has introduced legislation to lift the cap on income subject to Social Security taxes so the top 1 percent (those earning more than $250,000 a year) pay into the program as well. The same bill also increases Social Security benefits by about $65 a month for most recipients, increases cost-of-living adjustments, and provides a minimum Social Security benefit to significantly reduce the senior poverty rate.   —J.T.

From Bernie's marathon
Senate floor speech, December 10, 2010[27]

For all of us who understand that Social Security is life and death for tens of millions of Americans today and will be vitally important for working people as they reach retirement age, it is important that we understand that Social Security has done a great job. . . . Social Security, in my view, has been the most successful Federal program in perhaps the history of our country. In the last 75 years, whether in good or bad times, Social Security has paid out every nickel owed to every eligible American. Today, Social Security has a $2.6 trillion surplus. Today, Social Security can pay out benefits for the next 29 years. Our goal, and what we must do, is make sure we extend it beyond 29 years, for the next 75 years. Well, if we divert $120 billion from the Social Security trust fund and give it to workers today, what you are doing is cutting back the viability—the long-term viability—of Social Security. We want to make it stronger.

When the average Social Security benefit is just $1,328 a month, and more than one-third of our senior citizens rely on Social Security for virtually all of their income, our job must be to expand benefits, not cut them. The way to do that is to eliminate the cap on all income above $250,000 so that millionaires and billionaires pay the same percentage of their income into Social Security as middle-class Americans.

From Bernie's statement about the annual report from the Social Security trustees, May 31, 2013[28]

The report from the Social Security trustees confirms what many of us have known, that Social Security is not "going broke," that it can pay every benefit owed to every eligible American for the next 20 years and that after 2033 there is enough in reserve to pay three-quarters of future benefits.

Our job now is to make sure Social Security is strong not just for 20 years but for generations to come. The best way to do that is not to cut Social Security cost-of-living adjustments as Republicans and President Obama have proposed, but to do what Obama called for as a candidate in 2008. We must lift the cap on Social Security payroll taxes and make the wealthy contribute the same percentage of their income as other workers. Today, someone making $10 million a year contributes the same amount of money as someone making $113,700. That is absurd.

Bernie's Senate floor speech denouncing so-called reforms of Social Security, June 27, 2012[29]

And my friends back home, when you hear folks talking about Social Security reform, hold on to your wallets because they are talking about cuts in Social Security. Nothing more, nothing less. They're talking about something that in Vermont, nobody has heard of, the concept called chained CPI.

Every time I go home, I ask them. People don't know what chained CPI is. The so-called chained CPI is the belief—and I know senior citizens back home are going to start laughing when I say this—that COLAs [cost of living adjustments] for Social Security are too high. And seniors back home start scratching their heads and say wait, we just went through two years when my prescription drug costs went up, my health care costs went up and I got no COLA and there are people in Washington, Republicans, some Democrats, they think my COLA was too high?

What world are these people living in?

And that's the reality. So some of the folks here want to pass something called a chained CPI, which, if it were imposed—and I will do everything I can to see that it does not get imposed—would mean that between the ages of 65 and 75, a senior would lose about $560 a year, and then when they turn 85 and they're trying to get by off of $13,000 or $14,000 a year, they would lose about a thousand bucks a year. That's what some of our colleagues want to do. Virtually all the Republicans want to do it. Some Democrats want to do it as well. As chairman of the Defending Social Security Caucus, I'm going to do everything that I can to prevent that. Now, they also want to cut Medicare and they want to cut Medicaid. Well, we've got 50 million people without any health insurance at all. We've got people paying huge deductibles. Medicaid covering nursing home care. They want to cut Medicare and Medicaid. They have the brilliant idea, some of them, that maybe we should raise the retirement age for Medicare from 65 to 67.

Mr. President, tell me about somebody in Minnesota who's 66 and is diagnosed with cancer, and if we do what the Republicans want us to do in the House, which is to create a voucher plan for

Medicare, we'd give that person a check for, I don't know, $7,000 I think or $8,000 and say, you can go out to a private insurance company—anyone you want—here's your $7,000 or $8,000, you're suffering with cancer, go get your insurance. And I guess that would last you maybe one day or two days in the hospital. That's what it would do. That's the Republican plan. So, Mr. President, I agree that deficit reduction is a real issue and I think we have got to deal with it. But we are not, if I have anything to say about it, going to deal with it on the backs of the elderly, the children, the sick, the poor and the hungry. The way you deal with deficit reduction in a responsible way, in a fair way is you say to the billionaires in this country, who are doing phenomenally well, that there's something a little bit absurd that millionaires and billionaires today, in the midst of the deficit crisis, are paying the lowest tax rates that they have paid in decades.

So, yes, we're going to have to ask the wealthiest people in this country to start paying their fair share of taxes. I saw a piece in the paper the other day. It was quite incredible. Some billionaires apparently are leaving America, they're giving up their citizenship, and they're going abroad. These great lovers of America who made their money in this country, when you ask them to start paying their fair share of taxes, they're running abroad. We have 19-year-old kids in this country who've died in Iraq and Afghanistan defending this country, they went abroad not to escape taxes, they're working-class kids who died in wars and now some billionaires want to run abroad in order to avoid paying their fair share of taxes. What patriotism, what love of country. So, Mr. President, yeah, we've got to deal with deficit reduction. But you don't cut Social Security, you don't cut Medicare, you don't cut Medicaid, you don't cut education.

From an interview with the author, *Playboy*, November 2013[30]

The Business Roundtable—CEOs of the largest companies in the U.S.—came to Washington earlier this year and proposed that we raise the Medicare and Social Security eligibility ages to 70. Can you imagine the chutzpah of guys who are worth hundreds of millions of dollars in some cases and have retirement packages the likes of which average Americans couldn't even dream, proposing that? Can you imagine somebody who will get a golden parachute of perhaps tens of millions of dollars—who is not going to have a financial worry in his or her life—coming to Washington and saying, 'I want you to raise Medicare eligibility to 70?'" . . . These are people whose kids live in gated communities, people who get into their chauffeured cars when they travel, into their own jet planes, and go all over the world. They eat at the finest restaurants; they work out in the greatest gyms. They haven't got a clue or a concern about what's going on with ordinary Americans.

Bernie Facts

- Bernie cosponsored the 2013 Keeping Our Social Security Promises Act (S.500), which would eliminate the cap subject to payroll taxes on earned income above $250,000.

- In March 2015, backed by petitions from two million Americans, Bernie introduced the Social Security Expansion Act, which would increase Social Security benefits by about $65 a month for most recipients; increase cost-of-living adjustments; and provide a minimum Social Security benefit to significantly cut the senior poverty rate.

- Bernie fought Medicare and Medicaid cuts being considered by both parties in 2013, saying, "We're not going to balance the budget on the backs of the vulnerable."

10

Politics

Billionaires Cannot Buy Our Democracy

The Kochs are our homegrown oligarchs; they've cornered the market on Republican politics and are nakedly attempting to buy Congress and the White House.

—Tim Dickinson, *Rolling Stone*[31]

Proposing an amendment to the Constitution of the United States to expressly exclude for-profit corporations from the rights given to natural persons by the Constitution of the United States, prohibit corporate spending in all elections, and affirm the authority of Congress and the States to regulate corporations and to regulate and set limits on all election contributions and expenditures.

—proposed Saving American Democracy Amendment by Bernie Sanders and Representative Ted Deutch (D-FL)[32]

In 2010, the US Supreme Court ruled in *Citizens United v. Federal Election Commission*. Bernie has spoken out regularly about the case, calling it one of the worst decisions by the Supreme Court in the country's history. In *Citizens United*, the court ruled that "Political spending is a form of protected speech under the First Amendment, and the government may not keep corporations or unions from spending money to support or denounce individual candidates in elections. While corporations or unions may not give money directly to campaigns, they may seek to persuade the voting public through other means, including ads, especially where these ads were not broadcast."

Bernie believes the ruling put our democracy up for sale by destroying any limits on corporate spending and allowing billionaires to buy elections. It effectively considers a corporation a "person" by giving it the same free speech, First Amendment rights as an actual human being.

So Bernie has introduced a constitutional amendment in conjunction with Representative Ted Deutch, who is advocating the measure in the House. It must be passed by two-thirds of both the Senate and the House, and then ratified by three-fourths of the states (thirty-eight out of fifty). The proposed amendment reads as follows:

> SECTION 1. The rights protected by the Constitution of the United States are the rights of natural persons and do not extend to for-profit corporations, limited liability companies, or other private entities established for business purposes or to promote business interests under the laws of any state, the United States, or any foreign state.

> SECTION 2. Such corporate and other private entities established under law are subject to regulation by the people through the legislative process so long as such regulations are consistent with the powers of Congress and the States and do not limit the freedom of the press.

> SECTION 3. Such corporate and other private entities shall be prohibited from making contributions or expenditures in any election of any candidate for public office or the vote upon any ballot measure submitted to the people.

> SECTION 4. Congress and the States shall have the power to regulate and set limits on all election contributions and expenditures, including a candidate's own spending, and to authorize the establishment of political committees to receive, spend, and publicly disclose the sources of those contributions and expenditures.

—J.T.

From Bernie's Senate floor introduction of the constitutional amendment, December 8, 2011[33]

In my view, a corporation is not a person. In my view, a corporation does not have First Amendment rights, to spend as much money as it wants without disclosure, on a political campaign....

In my view, corporations should not be able to go into their treasuries, spend millions and millions of dollars, on a campaign, in order to buy elections.

I do not believe that that is what American democracy is supposed to be about.

I do not believe that that is what the bravest of the brave, from our country, fighting for democracy, fought and died to preserve....

Make no mistake: the *Citizens United* ruling has radically changed the nature of our democracy. Further tilting the balance of the power towards the rich and the powerful, at a time when already the wealthiest people in this country have never had it so good.

In my view, history will record, that the Supreme Court's *Citizens United* decision, is one of the worst decisions ever made by a Supreme Court, in the history of our country ... while the campaign finance system we had before Citizens United was, in my view, was a disaster ... as a result of Citizens United that bad situation has been made much worse....

According to an October 10th 2011 article in *Politico*, "the billionaire industrialist brothers David and Charles Koch plan to steer more than $200 million, potentially much more, to conservative groups ahead of Election Day 2012," ... Is that really the democracy that Americans fought and died for in war after war? I think not....

What happens here, on the floor of the Senate? ... The six largest banks on Wall Street have assets equal to over 65% of our GDP. Over $9 Trillion ... six banks.

Now when an issue comes up that impacts Wall Street, some of us, for example, think it might be a good idea to break up these huge banks. And members walk up to the desk up there and they have to decide. Am I going vote for this, am I going vote against it? With full knowledge, that if they vote against the interests of Wall Street, that two weeks later, there may be ads coming down into their state attacking them.

Every member of the Senate, every member of the House, in the back of their minds will be thinking, "Gee, if I cast the vote this way, if I take on some big money interest, am I going to be punished for that? Will a huge amount of money be unleashed in my state?" Everybody here understands that that's true.

It's not just taking on Wall Street, maybe it's taking on the drug companies, maybe it's taking on the private insurance companies, maybe it's taking on the military industrial complex.

But whatever powerful and wealthy special interest you are prepared to take on, on behalf of the interest of the middle class and working families of this country, when you walk up to that desk and you cast that vote, you know in the back of your mind, that you may be unleashing a tsunami of money coming into your state, and you're going to think twice about how you cast that vote.

We have go to send a Constitutional Amendment to the states that says simply and straightforwardly what everyone except five members of the United States Supreme Court seem to understand and that is corporations are not people. Bank of America is not a person. ExxonMobil is not a person.

From Bernie's speech at the National Press Club on March 9, 2015[34]

When the second wealthiest family in this country, with an extreme right wing agenda, and a few of their billionaire pals, have more political power than either of the two major political parties in this country, what is that political system called? Well, I think it should be called by its rightful name. It is not called democracy. It is called oligarchy. And that is the system we are rapidly moving toward. And that is a system we must vigorously oppose. . . .

Bernie Facts

- Bernie has pledged not to fund his campaign through Super PACS, which are vehicles to raise unlimited amounts of money that often cannot be tracked.

- Bernie has proposed a constitutional amendment to overturn *Citizens United*. He also supports efforts to create strong public financing of the election process.

- Bernie has also pledged, in the spirit of democracy, to continue his long-held practice of not running a single negative advertisement.

11

Infrastructure

Rebuild America

America's cumulative GPA for infrastructure rose slightly to a D+.... It is clear that we have a significant backlog of overdue maintenance across our infrastructure systems, a pressing need for modernization, and an immense opportunity to create reliable, long-term funding sources to avoid wiping out our recent gains.

—American Society of Civil Engineers,
2013 Report Card for America's Infrastructure[35]

Bernie has proposed spending $1 trillion over five years to fix the nation's crumbling infrastructure, which has been given a D+ grade by the American Society of Civil Engineers. His proposal would potentially create 13.5 million jobs for road crews, welders, engineers, and other workers who are looking for decent-paying, meaningful work. In introducing the plan, he said: "America once led the world in building and maintaining a nationwide network of safe and reliable bridges and roads. Today, nearly a quarter of the nation's 600,000 bridges have been designated as structurally deficient or functionally obsolete. Let's rebuild our crumbling infrastructure. Let's make our country safer and more efficient. Let's put millions of Americans back to work."

This isn't a new subject of interest for him. Five years ago, he underscored the nation's declining roads, bridges, and other infrastructure deficiencies in his sweeping speech on the Senate floor.   —J.T.

From Bernie's marathon
Senate floor speech, December 10, 2010[36]

I remember I was in Rutland, VT, the second or third largest city in the State of Vermont, and the mayor showed me a piece of pipe, an old piece of pipe.

He said: You know, the engineer who helped develop this water system and lay this pipe, after he did this work for Rutland, he went off to fight in the war.

I knew there was a catch line coming. I said: What war was it?

He said: It was the Civil War.

So you are talking about water pipe being in Rutland, VT—and this is true all over the United States—laid in the Civil War. The result is, we lose an enormous amount of clean water every day through leaks and water pipes bursting all over the United States of America. . . .

But we remain far behind most other countries around the industrialized world. China is exploding in terms of the number of high-speed rail lines they have. We have to do better. Our airports need work. Our air controllers need to be updated in terms of the technology they have and use to make our flights safe.

The point is, what most economists would tell you is when you invest in infrastructure, you get a bigger bang for the buck. You create more jobs for your investment than, in most instances, giving a variety of tax breaks to the corporate world.

Second of all, and not unimportantly, when you invest in infrastructure, you are improving the future of this country. You are making us more productive. It is not just creating jobs, it is creating jobs for very specific purposes, which makes our Nation more productive and efficient.

Bernie often compares the woeful state of US infrastructure with the progress being made in China. So what is China doing with its infrastructure? —J.T.

In China, they are investing almost four times our rate—or 9 percent—of their GDP annually in their infrastructure. Years ago, I was in Shanghai, China. I was coming from the airport to downtown as part of a congressional delegation. While we were on the bus coming in, my wife noticed something. She said: What was that? There was a blur that went by the window. Of course, I didn't notice it; she did. It turned out that blur was an experimental train they were working on—high-speed rail, which is now operational there, and other similar prototypes are being developed in China. Here we are, the United States of America, which for so many years led the world in so many ways, and now you are seeing a newly developing country such as China with high-speed rail all over their country, making them more productive and efficient, and in our cities, our subways are breaking down. Amtrak is going 50, 60 miles an hour, and the Chinese and Europeans have trains going hundreds of miles an hour. Yet if you drive around certain parts of America, you think we are a Third World nation. You have roads with all kinds of potholes. You have bridges, which you cannot go across. You have rail systems where trains are going slower—there is a study out there that I am going to get to later—where somebody said that decades and decades ago, it took less time to go from various parts of this country to the other on trains than it does today because our rail beds are in such bad shape.

Bernie's Senate floor speech about the need to invest in infrastructure, March 24, 2015[37]

I don't think there is a great debate on whether our infrastructure is crumbling. I don't think there is a great debate—and I speak as a former mayor—that if you allow your infrastructure to continue to crumble, it only becomes more expensive to rebuild it. I don't think there is a debate on that.

The debate, of course, comes down to how you pay for it. That debate has been going on here for many years. If anyone had a magical solution, I suspect it would have been brought forth already. But the proposal we are bringing forth calls for a $478 billion investment over a 6-year period. That will be paid for by eliminating some outrageous corporate loopholes today that, among other things, allow large, profitable corporations to stash their profits in the Cayman Islands, in Bermuda, and in other tax havens and not have to pay one nickel in taxes to the U.S. Government.

Our proposal is pretty simple. Let's eliminate some of those loopholes, let's take that money, let's invest in rebuilding our crumbling infrastructure, let's make our country more efficient, more productive, safer, and let us create millions of jobs. The need for rebuilding our infrastructure should not be in doubt. One out of every nine bridges in our country is structurally deficient, and nearly one-quarter are functionally obsolete. Almost one-third of our roads are in poor or mediocre condition. And as everybody stuck in a traffic jam at this moment knows, more than 42 percent of urban highways are congested.

Much of our rail network is obsolete. We are competing against countries which have high-speed rail, which operates much more rapidly than our railroads do. America's airports are bursting at the seams and still rely on antiquated 1960s radar technology. More than 4,000 of our Nation's dams are considered deficient, and nearly 9 percent of all levees are likely to fail during a major flood. That is a pretty scary proposition.

Our drinking water systems are nearing the end of their useful lives all over this country. Virtually every day there is another pipe which bursts, causing flooding in downtowns and wasting huge amounts of clean drinking water. Further, our wastewater plants routinely fail during heavy rains, allowing all kinds of crap to go into our lakes and our rivers, which should not be the case. Our aging electrical grid has hundreds of avoidable power failures each year and is unacceptably vulnerable to cyber attacks.

Now $478 billion may seem like a lot of money. It is a lot of money, but the American Society of Civil Engineers tells us we need to invest an additional $1.6 trillion to get our infrastructure into a state of good repair by 2020. To be honest with you, while this amendment is a significant step forward, it does not go anywhere near as far as it should go. I would hope on this amendment we would have strong bipartisan support. It is not good enough for people to continue to say what everybody acknowledges—yes, we need to rebuild our crumbling infrastructure, but, no, we don't know how we are going to come up with the money to do it. It is too late to keep expressing that rhetoric. We have heard it for too many years.

Every day we don't act, it becomes more expensive for us to act. . . . The time for rhetoric is gone. The time for action is now. Let's rebuild our crumbling infrastructure. Let's put people to work. Let's end outrageous corporate tax loopholes. Let's make our country safer, more efficient, and more productive.

Bernie Facts

- Bernie has proposed spending $1 trillion over five years to fix the nation's crumbling infrastructure.

- Bernie most recently attempted to make a down payment on that $1 trillion plan with a Senate push to approve $478 billion over six years that would be funded by closing corporate tax loopholes. The proposal came within a few votes of approval.

- In January 2015, Bernie pushed to advance infrastructure spending and link it to arresting climate change with a bill to "increase the quantity of solar photovoltaic electricity by providing rebates for the purchase and installation of an additional 10,000,000 photovoltaic systems by 2025."[38]

12

Veterans

Care for Them When They Come Home

He works for veterans. He's not just saying that. He does do the work.

—Brenda Cruickshank, retired army nurse
and immediate past commander of the Vermont
Veterans of Foreign Wars in *Politico*, July 2, 2015[39]

He is revered. He's very consistent with where he stands. He's the first politician that I've believed in my life.

—Paul Loebe, a thirty-one-year-old who served in both
Iraq and Afghanistan during eight years of active duty[40]

Going back to his days in the House of Representatives, Bernie paid special attention to the needs of military veterans. Though often opposing military adventurism (he was a vocal opponent of the Iraq War), Bernie has always believed that veterans deserve the best possible treatment upon finishing their service, particularly when it comes to the benefits managed by the Veterans Administration, including health care.

Bernie's passion for veterans was best seen when he fought, as chairman of the Senate Committee on Veterans' Affairs, to pass the Comprehensive Veterans Health and Benefits and Military Retirement Pay Restoration Act of 2014 but was blocked by Republicans.   —J.T.

Bernie's Senate floor speech, February 27, 2014[41]

If a Member of the Senate wants to look that veteran in the eyes and say to him or her that they think we cannot afford to help that individual who sacrificed so much for this country have a family, well go do that. Tell that individual that you think we cannot afford to help him or her, but when you do that, I hope you will also tell him why you voted to give $1 trillion in tax breaks to the top 2 percent at a time when the wealthiest people in this country are doing phenomenally well. Virtually all of my Republican colleagues thought it was appropriate to provide huge tax breaks to millionaires and billionaires.

So when you speak to that young veteran who can no longer have a child and you are going to explain why we cannot afford to help that family, tell them it was OK to vote for tax breaks for the Koch brothers or the Walton family, but we do not have enough money to help them start a family.

If you as a Senator see a 70-year-old woman or 75-year-old woman pushing a wheelchair for a veteran who lost his legs in Vietnam, tell that woman, have the courage, have the honesty to tell that woman we cannot extend the caregiver benefits to her that we have, quite appropriately, for the post-9/11 veterans. Tell that woman who may be taking care of that disabled vet 7 days a week, 24 hours a day, who lives under enormous stress, that we do not have the resources to help her with a modest stipend; we do not have the resources as the U.S. Government to maybe have a nurse come in once a week to relieve her. We do not have the resources to give her some technical help for herself, for her husband. Explain to her that we cannot afford to do that.

But then in the same breath, if you please, explain how you can support a situation where one out of four corporations in this country does not pay a nickel in Federal income taxes. It is OK for General Electric, some of the largest corporations in the world in a given year, not to pay a penny in Federal income tax, but we somehow do not have the money to give a little bit of help to a 70-, 75-year-old wife who is working 24/7 to give support to their loved ones.

I say to my follow Senators: If you happen to meet a veteran who is trying to get by on $28,000, $30,000, $35,000 a year, and you notice that the teeth in his mouth are rotting, if you notice that person may not have health insurance, one of the million veterans in this country who have no health insurance, I want you to go up to that veteran and have the courage, the honesty, to tell them that you believe the United States of America does not have the money to take care of his needs, to get him VA health care, to help him fix his teeth.

But explain to him why you may have voted for more than $100 billion in tax breaks for the wealthiest three-tenths of 1 percent because you think we should repeal the estate tax that only applies to the wealthiest three-tenths of 1 percent, the wealthiest of the wealthy. You are prepared to vote, and virtually all Republicans are, to give millionaire and billionaire families, the wealthiest of the wealthy, the top three-tenths of 1 percent, $100 billion in tax breaks, but we are not prepared, we supposedly do not have the money to get VA health care for someone making $28,000, $30,000 or dental care for someone whose teeth are rotting in his mouth.

You go explain that. Have the honesty, the courage, guys, to say: Yes, tax breaks for billionaires, but we do not have the resources to get you into VA health care. I want you to explain to a young woman who left the military, maybe broken in spirit because she was raped or sexually assaulted while in the military, tell her America does not have the resources to get her, through the VA, the proper care she needs to get her life back together after her sexual assault. Tell her that.

If you happen to meet a young man who was eligible for the post-9/11 GI bill, who today cannot afford to go to college where he lives because he is not eligible for in-state tuition and there is a gap between what the GI education bill pays and what is required in the State he is living in of $10,000, he cannot afford it, cannot go to college, explain to him that we do not have the money to help him.

If you bump into an old veteran—we have heard some discussion in the last couple of days that the VA lacks adequate health care facilities, we do not have enough around the country. This legislation that we are voting on right now, that in fact was already passed in the House, provides for the VA to enter into leases for 27 medical facilities all across this country in 18 different States.

Tell him, tell that 70-year-old veteran or the 80-year-old veteran who wants access to primary health care near where he lives that we do not have the resources to provide that primary care, but we can spend billions of dollars rebuilding the infrastructure in Afghanistan, where most of that money is stolen by a corrupt leadership.

Maybe, colleagues, one of you will see a young veteran, one of hundreds of thousands of veterans of Iraq and Afghanistan who are dealing with PTSD or traumatic brain injury or maybe it is a young man who has come back who just cannot find a job in this very tough economy. Go up to him and say: Yes, tax breaks for the rich are great; corporations not paying taxes, that is OK, but I do not believe we should be providing help to you.

When Bernie was successful at blocking attempts in the Senate in 2013 to cut benefits for disabled veterans, he spoke passionately about his position, as you can see from this following quote in a news article. —J.T.

The time has come for the Senate to send a very loud and clear message to the American people: We will not balance the budget on the backs of disabled veterans who have lost their arms, their legs and their eyesight defending our country. We will not balance the budget on the backs of the men and women who have already sacrificed for us in Iraq and Afghanistan, nor on the widows who have lost their husbands in Iraq and Afghanistan defending our country.[42]

From an interview with the author, *Playboy*, November 2013[43]

People who give great speeches about the need to go to war and years later talk about gutting benefits for vets or ignoring their needs? As somebody who has always been antiwar—I'm not a pacifist but I've always understood war is the last recourse—I also understand the cost of war. Some people think more Vietnam vets committed suicide than were killed in Vietnam. Lives were just totally destroyed. Right now, as a result of this war in Iraq, which I voted against, there are an estimated 50,000 veterans suffering from minor to moderate traumatic brain injuries. These are folks you would not recognize walking down the street. This is not somebody who has had half his head blown off. These are folks who are functioning but have been exposed to multiple explosions; maybe they have had many, many concussions. We don't know what that will mean over the years. We don't know its impact on depression, on other emotional attributes, on behavior.

Bernie Facts

- Bernie proposed an amendment in March 2013, that blocked cuts in benefits for disabled veterans. The cuts would have meant, according to the Veterans Advantage website,[44] "Veterans who started receiving VA disability benefits at age 30 would have their benefits reduced by $1,425 at age 45, $2,341 at age 55 and $3,231 at age 65. Benefits for more than 350,000 surviving spouses and children who have lost a loved one in battle also would be cut."

- Bernie steered, as chairman of the Senate Committee on Veterans' Affairs, landmark legislation in 2014 to increase the Department of Veterans Affairs' ability to serve America's aging population of veterans and handle a new generation of men and women who served in Iraq and Afghanistan. The legislation, Veterans Access, Choice, and Accountability Act of 2014, passed the Senate 93–3 after passing the House 265–160 and was signed by President Obama on August 7, 2014. The law included $5 billion for the VA to hire more doctors and other health care professionals.

- Bernie previously attempted to push through the Comprehensive Veterans Health and Benefits and Military Retirement Pay Restoration Act of 2014, a $21 billion package that would have improved a whole set of benefits for vets. The bill was blocked by Republicans.

13

Agriculture

Our Food, Our Farmers, Our Health

*Bernie Sanders has his sleeves rolled up and he's going after
one of the big "bullies" in the dairy industry.*
—Pete Hardin, *The Milkweed*, August 2009[45]

Bernie has been a fierce advocate for the small farmer, not a surprise
given that Vermont's dairy industry is the source of income for many
people in that rural state. Because dairy prices have been pummeled,
Bernie has been particularly attuned to the almost one thousand
dairy farms dotting the state. But he has looked for policy solutions
that tackle a crisis affecting dairy farms nationwide, including taking
on large corporate dairy operations whose anti-competitive practices
hurt regular farmers and consumers.

At the same time, Bernie has viewed farm issues broadly,
including his thoughts on the concerns people voice about genetically modified organisms (GMOs) in foods. In the most recent
five-year, massive Farm Bill passed by Congress, Bernie proposed a
simple amendment to allow states to require labeling of all products using GMOs.   —J.T.

Bernie's Senate floor speech
supporting dairy farmers, August 4, 2009[46]

All of us know that today our country is in a major economic crisis,
the deepest recession since the Great Depression. But sometimes
what media does, and maybe what we do here in Congress, is focus on
that crisis in the areas where there is, if you like, concentrated misery,
such as Detroit, which has undergone terrible problems, thousands
of people on a given day have lost their jobs, and sometimes, in the

midst of the economic crisis facing our country, we forget what is happening in rural areas, in small towns all over this country.

Sometimes when farms go out of business, farms that have been owned by a family for generations, when rural communities go into, literally, an economic depression, we don't pay quite as much [attention] to that. It is not on the front pages of the *New York Times*. The fact is, right now rural America is in the midst of a very serious economic crisis. Unemployment is extremely high.

One of the particular areas where we are seeing not just a deep recession but, in fact, a depression is within the dairy industry. In the last year, if you can believe it, the price dairy farmers—many of them small, family-based dairy farmers—have received for their milk has plummeted by 41 percent. In the last year, it has gone down by 41 percent. The reality of what that means is that farmers today, for every gallon of milk they are producing, are losing money. It is not that they are making a little bit, they are losing money. What we are seeing, not just in the Northeast, not just in the Midwest, not just in the Southeast, not just in the West, but all over this country, are family farmers going out of business, plunging their rural economies and their communities into depression-type economics

Let me quote, if I might, from people from different parts of the country.

A Minnesota dairy farmer writes:

> This situation is unlike any experienced in the past and the width and depth cannot continue to be ignored. It has not discriminated based on herd size or geographic location. Dairy farmers of all sizes and across all regions of the country are enduring an unprecedented disaster.

That is from Minnesota. The President of the California Farmers Union—when we talk about dairy, sometimes California is in another world from the rest of the country because their herds are much larger. . . . This is what the fellow who is the head of the California Farmer's Union says. His name is Joaquin Contente. He testified:

[I]n my lifetime history as a dairy farmer, I have never seen our prices remain this far below our costs this long and I have never seen so many dairy producers so desperate for relief. In my county alone 25 dairies have either filed or are in the process of filing for bankruptcy and many more are closer to bankruptcy each day.

From Texas, the executive director of the Texas Association of Dairymen said:

This is the worst situation I have seen since 1970. Some say it is the worst since the Depression.

From Wisconsin, a dairy farmer states:

In my area farmers are burning up the equity accumulated over their lifetimes. One farmer in my area had to cash out his wife's IRA just to get his crops planted this spring. My parish priest in my small town has had to counsel one or more dairy farmers a week to prevent their suicides.

Those are just a few examples from Wisconsin, California, and Texas. Trust me, I could tell you many similar stories from the State of Vermont. Once again, as we attempt to revitalize our economy, let's not forget about rural America. Let's not forget about dairy farmers.

Bernie's Senate floor speech supporting his amendment to require labeling of GMOs, May 22, 2013[47]

Monsanto and the other biotech companies spent something like $47 million against the right of people of California to have labeling on GMO products, and they won. The people who support labeling got 47 percent of the vote despite a huge amount of money being spent against them.

In the State of Washington, over 300,000 people have signed petitions in support of an initiative there to label genetically engineered food in that State.

A poll done earlier this year indicated that some 82 percent of the American people believe labeling should take place with regard to genetically engineered ingredients.

This is a pretty simple issue, and the issue is do the American people have a right to know what they are eating, what is in the food they are ingesting and what their kids are eating. . . .

Genetically engineered food labels will not increase costs to shoppers, as we all know. Companies change their labels every day. They market their products differently. Adding a label does not change this. Everybody looks at labels. They change all the time. This would simply be an addition, new information on that label. In fact, many products already voluntarily label their food as GMO-free.

Further, genetically engineered crops are not better for the environment. Some will say, well, this is good for the environment. The use of Monsanto Roundup-ready soybeans engineered to withstand exposure to the herbicide Roundup has caused the spread of Roundup-resistant weeds which now infest 22 States, 10 million acres in 22 States, with predictions for 40 million acres or more by mid-decade. Resistant weeds increase the use of herbicides and the use of older and more toxic herbicides.

Further, there are no international agreements that permit the mandatory identification of foods produced through genetic engineering. As I mentioned earlier, throughout Europe and in dozens of other countries around the world, this exists. It is not a very radical concept. It exists throughout the European Union and I believe, very simply, that States in this country should be able to go forward in labeling genetically modified foods if they want, and this amendment simply makes it clear they have the right to do that."

Bernie Facts

- Bernie's August 2009 amendment increased the budget for the Farm Service Agency by $350 million to help struggling small dairy farmers survive a huge drop in prices created by pressure from large dairy conglomerates.

- Bernie came to the defense of small dairy farmers, demanding that the US Department of Justice investigate anti-competitive actions by Dean Foods, the nation's largest fluid milk processor.

- Bernie led the fight, with an amendment in a massive farm bill, for a GMO-labeling provision that would have allowed states to require that any food, beverage, or other edible product offered for sale have a label indicating whether or not it contains a genetically engineered ingredient.

14

Immigration

Keep the American Dream Alive

The DREAM Act is really about hard work, fairness, education and parents making sacrifices for their children so that way they can have a better life.

—Flavia de la Fuenta, student, California[48]

Bernie, like millions of Americans, is the son of an immigrant family. He has often said that the story of today's immigrants is the story of his life. From that experience, Bernie has been motivated to strongly support a comprehensive immigration bill, including the Development, Relief, and Education for Alien Minors [DREAM] Act, to protect workers and their families and grant citizenship to millions of people who work hard in the shadows of the economy, particularly millions of Latino workers and their families.

Bernie has also been clear that immigration reform cannot allow corporations to exploit workers. He has regularly pointed out that corporate advocates for immigration overhaul include Motorola, Dell, Hewlett-Packard, IBM, Microsoft, Intel, and Boeing, which have outsourced hundreds of thousands of jobs overseas and have announced major layoffs of thousands of American workers. Those companies, Bernie says, have to be prevented from pushing through immigration laws that advance a cost-cutting, anti-worker agenda.   —J.T.

Bernie's speech to the National Association of Latino Elected and Appointed Officials, June 19, 2015[49]

It is no great secret that across the United States undocumented workers perform a critical role in our economy. They harvest and process our food and it is no exaggeration to say that, without them, food production in the United States would significantly decline. Undocumented workers build many of our homes, cook our meals, maintain our landscapes. We even entrust undocumented workers with that which we hold most dear—our children.

Despite the central role they play in our economy and in our daily lives, undocumented workers are reviled by many for political gain and shunted into the shadows. . . . It is time for this disgraceful situation to end. This country faces enormous problems and they will not be solved unless we are united. It is time to end the politics of division on this country, of politicians playing one group of people against another: white against black, male against female, straight against gay, native born against immigrant.

That is why I supported the 2013 comprehensive immigration reform legislation in the United States Senate. While a complicated piece of comprehensive legislation like this can always be improved I believed then and now that it is time to end the discussion of mass deportation or self-deportation. We cannot and we should not even be talking about sweeping up millions of men, women, and children—many of whom have been here for years—and throwing them out of the country. That's wrong and that type of discussion has got to end. . . .

I strongly support the Administration's Deferred Action for Childhood Arrivals (DACA) program. DACA a good first step, but should be expanded. Deferred action should include the parents of citizens, parents of legal permanent residents, and the parents of DREAMERs. We should be pursuing policies that unite families—not tear them apart.

I continue to be a strong supporter of the DREAM Act, which would offer the opportunity of permanent residency and eventual citizenship to young people who were brought to the United States as children. It is my belief that we should recognize the young men and women who comprise the DREAMers for what they are—American kids who deserve the right to legally be in the country they know as home.

As is often said, we are a nation of immigrants. For generations, families braved treacherous paths, often fleeing unspeakable poverty and violence, in search of better futures, for better lives for their children.

I, myself, am the son of an immigrant. My father came to this country from Poland at the age of 17 without a nickel in his pocket and without much of an education. Like immigrants before and since, he worked hard to give his family a better life here in the United States. He was a paint salesman and we were solidly lower-middle class. My parents, my brother and I lived together in a small rent-controlled apartment in Brooklyn, New York. My mother's wish—which she never realized—was that we would be able to buy a house of our own and move out of that small apartment. Through my parents' hard work both my brother and I went to college.

Their story, my story, our story is a story of America. Hard working families coming to the United States to create a brighter future for their children. It is a story rooted in family and fueled by hope. It is a story that continues to this day in families all across the United States.

Let me tell you that I have seen first-hand the impact of our broken immigration system. In 2008, my U.S. Senate office learned about a crisis occurring with migrant laborers in the tomato fields of Immokalee, Florida. The Immokalee workers were fighting to increase the paltry wages they were receiving for back-breaking work.

Although far from Vermont, in January of 2008, I decided to go there myself and investigate . . . what I found was a human tragedy. Workers were being paid starvation wages, living in severely substandard housing, and subjected to abusive labor practices. The injustice in the lives of the workers was overwhelming.

In fact, the situation was so bad that on the day I visited two men were indicted for human slavery. Slavery in the 21st century in the United States of America. . . .

I am happy to tell you that this story has a positive ending. The campaign by the Immokalee workers resulted in substantial reforms in the tomato fields of Florida. In the aggregate, workers there have seen their wages increase by millions of dollars and improvement in their working conditions.

But how many more Immokalees are out there? How many fields or factories are there where people—often without legal status—are used up and thrown away? We cannot continue to run an economy where millions are made so vulnerable because of their undocumented status. We have to ask ourselves. Whose interest is it in to keep undocumented workers in the shadows without the protection of the law?

Many in the business community have argued for guest worker programs as the answer to the immigration issue. This concerns me very much.

As the Southern Poverty Law Center has documented, guest workers have been routinely cheated out of wages; held virtually captive by employers who have seized their documents; forced to live in unspeakably inhumane conditions; and denied medical benefits for on-the-job injuries. That is unacceptable.

In the U.S. Senate, I have introduced legislation in 2007 that would authorize the Legal Services Corporation to provide legal representation to guest workers who have been abused by their employers. Further, employers under my bill would be required to reimburse guest workers for transportation expenses and provide workers' compensation insurance, among other things.

I also opposed tying immigration reform to the building of a border fence. Let me say what most people already know. Undocumented workers come to the United States to escape economic hardship and political persecution.

Undocumented workers looking for economic opportunity come to the United States because there are no jobs where they are coming from, and there are jobs for them here. Plain and simple. . . .

Since the implementation of NAFTA, the number of Mexicans living below the poverty line has increased by over 14 million people. Almost 2 million small famers have been displaced. And in the twenty years since NAFTA growth in per capita GDP has been only half of that experienced by other Latin American nations. Not surprisingly we have seen a 185 percent increase in the number of undocumented immigrants from Mexico from 1992 to 2011.

We as a nation have got to realize the importance of dealing not just with the issue of immigration but with the very real refugee crisis we face. It was appalling to me that last year when the papers were full of discussion of the large numbers of unaccompanied children at the borders there were so many voices insisting they be turned away or simply shipped back to their country of origin like a package marked return to sender. America has always been a haven for the oppressed. Is there any group more vulnerable than children? We cannot and must not shirk the historic role of the United States as a protector of vulnerable people fleeing persecution.

The bottom line of all of this is that it is time to bring our neighbors out of the shadows. It is time to give them legal status. It is time to create a reasonable and responsible path to citizenship.

In addition to immigration reform, we must also pursue policies that empower minority communities. This must start with energizing Latinos all across the country to engage in the democratic process and by thwarting efforts to disenfranchise minority voters. Restricting access through draconian voter ID laws and shortening early voting periods are thinly-veiled efforts to marginalize communities of color, low income people and seniors. These policies must be combated at both the state and federal levels.

But to truly empower our communities, we must address the crippling poverty that affects tens of millions of people in this country. Today, shamefully, we have more than 12 million Latinos living in poverty. That's nearly one out of every four Latinos in this country. If you are a Latino child, there is nearly a one in three chance (32 percent) that you are growing up in poverty.

Many of those in poverty are working at low-wage jobs. These are the people who struggle every day to find the money to feed their kids, to pay their electric bills and to put gas in the car to get to work.

I believe we need a major federal jobs program to put millions of Americans back to work. One in four construction workers are Latino, and the fastest way to increase jobs is to rebuild our crumbling infrastructure: roads, bridges, water systems, waste water plants, airports, railroads and schools. It has been estimated that the cost of the Iraq War, a war we should never have waged, will total . . . $4–6 trillion by the time the last veteran receives needed care. A $1 trillion investment in infrastructure would create 13 million decent paying jobs and make this country more efficient, productive and safer.

We also need to address the crisis of youth unemployment. The real unemployment rate for young Hispanic college graduates is 11%, nearly double the rate of white Americans. For young Hispanics with only a high school degree, the real unemployment rate is 36%.

More than 50,000 Latinos turn 18 every month, and the time is long overdue for us to start investing in our young people, to help them get the jobs and training they need, the education they deserve, so that they can be part of the middle class. It's time to bring opportunity to communities across the country. I recently introduced legislation to provide $5.5 billion in immediate funding to States and localities to employ 1 million young Americans between the ages of 16 and 24, and provide job training to hundreds of thousands of other young Americans.

We must also finally address the greed, recklessness and illegal behavior of Wall Street. Financial institutions cannot be an island unto themselves, standing as huge profit centers outside of the real economy. Their speculation and illegal behavior plunged this country into the worst financial crisis since the 1930s, and Latinos were the hardest hit. Latinos were disproportionately steered into subprime loans and around a quarter of Latino borrowers have lost their homes to foreclosure or are seriously delinquent. In my view, Wall Street is too large and powerful to be reformed. The huge financial institutions must be broken up.

In today's highly competitive global economy, millions of Americans are unable to afford the higher education they need in order to get good-paying jobs. Some of our young people have given up the dream of going to college, while others are leaving school deeply in debt. Many of the countries we compete with understand that free public education should not end at high school. In many European countries, students leave college debt free. That should be the case here in our country. I've introduced legislation to make all public colleges in this country tuition free.

What we need to do is invest in the Latino community so that America can reach its full potential. I'm proud to stand with the Latino community and receive a 100% voting score from the National Hispanic Leadership Agenda last Congress.

Bernie Facts

- Bernie has strongly supported comprehensive immigration reform, including the DREAM Act.

- Bernie introduced legislation in 2007 that would authorize the Legal Services Corporation to provide legal representation to guest workers who have been abused by their employers.

- Bernie continues to fight against NAFTA-style trade deals that impoverish workers and force people off their lands, putting them at great risk of exploitation by large corporations because of their undocumented status.

15

Civil Rights
The Long Road to Justice

It's official I support @SenSanders! His call 4 the restoration of the voters rights act sealed the deal for me . . . I am beginning to see American political families like monarchs and I have no affection for monarchs.
—Rapper Killer Mike of Run the Jewels via Twitter[50]

Bernie Sanders entered into politics through the civil rights movement, working more than a half century ago as a civil rights activist in the 1960s. He organized with the Congress of Racial Equality (CORE) in Chicago and led a sit-in against segregated housing in 1962. Amazingly, he is one of only two sitting US senators to have attended the 1963 March on Washington, and he saw Dr. Martin Luther King Jr. give his "I Have a Dream" speech. He engineered a 1988 primary victory in Vermont for the Reverend Jesse Jackson Sr., who was viewed as an insurgent candidate running on a populist platform similar to Sanders' current positions.   —J.T.

—On Racism—
Bernie's speech to the
National Council of La Raza, July 13, 2015[51]

Racism has plagued this country for centuries. We should be proud, however, that in recent decades, we have made significant progress, real progress, in overcoming racism and in defeating it; in creating a country where we judge people, as Martin Luther King Jr. reminded us, not on the color of their skin. Not on the language they speak. Not on the country where they came from. But on their character and qualities as human beings. . . .

We are making progress in the country and there will be no turning back. And let me be very clear in stating that no one—not Donald Trump, not anyone else—will be successful dividing us on race or our country of origin. . . .

America becomes a greater nation, a stronger nation, when we stand together as one people and in a very loud and clear voice, we say no to all forms of racism and bigotry. . . .

Last but not least, think of a nation where every person in this country—no matter their race, no matter their country of origin, no matter their religion, no matter their disability, no matter their sexual orientation—that all come together, to create the greatest country that anyone has even seen; a country that works for all of our people, and we do it when we stand together, and we do not allow people to divide us, divide us, divide us.

Bernie has always been acutely aware of the deep stain of racism in America and how non-white communities, particularly African Americans, are the targets of police violence and unemployment. He talks about this in his NPR interview, but it was also evident when he introduced legislation in 2014, and again in 2015, to spend billions on youth employment programs, specifically in poor communities and communities of color.   —J.T.

From an interview with
National Public Radio, June 25, 2015[52]

It means we are not going to accept police brutality or illegal behavior against young African Americans OR anybody else. But when you talk about "lives matter," sometimes what we forget is when 51 percent of young African-American kids are unemployed. Are those lives that matter? . . .

Black lives matter; white lives matter; Hispanic lives matter. But these are also not only police matters, they're not only gun control matters, they are significantly economic matters. . . . Because it's too easy for quote-unquote liberals to be saying, "Well, let's use this phrase." Well, what are we going to do about 51 percent of young African Americans unemployed? . . .

We need a massive jobs program to put black kids to work and white kids to work and Hispanic kids to work. So my point is, is that it's sometimes easy to say—worry about what phrase you're going to use. It's a lot harder to stand up to the billionaire class and say, "You know what? You're going to have to pay some taxes. You can't get away with putting your money in tax havens, because we need that money to create millions of jobs for black kids, for white kids, for Hispanic kids."

In 2015, Bernie took to the floor[53] urging leaders in South Carolina to take down the Confederate flag from the grounds of its state capitol, noting that it was a relic of our nation's "stained racial history," a theme he's reprised on the campaign trail. —J.T.

[I]n the last 60 years this country has made significant progress on civil rights. 60 years ago, parts of our country were built on an apartheid-type system: segregated housing, segregated schools, segregated restaurants, segregated transportation, segregated water fountains and an entire segregated way of life. Perhaps most significantly African Americans in a number of southern states were denied the right to vote and were unable to participate in the Democratic Process.

Today, we have a right to be proud of the significant changes that have taken place in our country, and the many advances that have been made in civil rights and in the creation of a less discriminatory society. We should be proud that in 2008 this country surprised the world by overcoming its racist history and electing our first African American president and then re-electing him four years later with a strong majority. . . .

But clearly, while we have made significant progress, the events of last week remind us how far we yet have to go in order to create a non-racist society.

Mr. President, I am not the governor of South Carolina, I am not in the South Carolina legislature and I do not live in South Carolina. But I do believe that the time is long overdue for the people of South Carolina to remove the Confederate flag from the state house grounds in Columbia.

That flag is a relic of our nation's stained racial history. It should come down. . . . Frankly, the Confederate flag does not belong on state house grounds. It belongs in a museum.

Mr. President, let me also express to you my deep concern about the growth of extremist groups in this country, who are motivated by hatred—by hatred of African Americans, by hatred of immigrants, by hatred of Jews, by hatred of Muslims, and anyone else who is not exactly like them. Mr. President, sadly, according to the Southern Poverty Law Center, there are some 784 active hate groups in the United States. And the number of those groups [is] growing. Let me express my agreement with NAACP President Cornell William Brooks that "we need vigorous prosecution and vigorous investigation of these hate groups and the resources to do so."

Mr. President, about 50 years ago as a student at the University of Chicago, I was arrested in the civil rights demonstration to end segregated schools. I was also involved in helping to end segregated housing in Chicago. Mr. President, let me end by reminding you of those great words in the American Declaration of Independence. "We hold these truths to be self-evident that all men are created equal, that they are endowed by their creator with certain unalienable rights, that among these are life, liberty and the pursuit of happiness." Mr. President, that is the dream of America and that is the goal that we must strive towards. The tragedy in Charleston reminds us all how far we still have to go.

Bernie Facts

- As a young man, Bernie was a civil rights activist, a passion that drew him to the 1963 March on Washington, where he saw Dr. Martin Luther King Jr. give his "I Have a Dream" speech. He has campaigned relentlessly against racism, which he links to the high levels of unemployment in non-white communities.

- On June 4, 2015, Sanders, along with Representative John Conyers (D-MI), proposed the Employ Young Americans Now Act to combat growing incarceration rates by providing jobs to young people. The bill would create a $5.5 billion fund in order to employ one million young adults between the ages of sixteen and twenty-four. In 2014, when Sanders introduced similar legislation, he said, "If we are serious about solving the economic crisis facing our young people today, instead of providing police departments with free military equipment, it would be a much better use of our resources to create the jobs that young Americans desperately need. It is a much better investment for our society to create jobs for young Americans than it is to throw them in jail."[54]

16

Foreign Policy
Peace and Diplomacy, Not War

*He really does say what he believes, and just seeing how
people respond to that, I wanted to be part of it.*

—Benjamin Powell, eighteen, Dedham, Massachusetts[55]

Sanders has been a longtime opponent of military intervention. He
voted against the Iraq War, has criticized bloated defense budgets,
and is generally opposed to military conflict. He supports the current negotiated deal with Iran to halt the spread of nuclear weapons,
calling it "a victory for diplomacy over saber-rattling and could keep
the United States from being drawn into another never-ending war
in the Middle East." He also has been an advocate for a just peace in
the Palestine–Israel conflict, urging the United States, as far back as
1988, to use its clout and threat of cutting off support to Israel to
reach an agreement. —J.T.

Bernie's House floor speech during the debate over
the authorization to go to war in Iraq, October 9, 2002[56]

I do not think any Member of this body disagrees that Saddam
Hussein is a tyrant, a murderer, and a man who has started two
wars. He is clearly someone who cannot be trusted or believed. The
question, Mr. Speaker, is not whether we like Saddam Hussein or
not. The question is whether he represents an imminent threat to the
American people and whether a unilateral invasion of Iraq will do
more harm than good. . . .

[T]he front page of *The Washington Post* today reported that all
relevant U.S. intelligence agencies now say despite what we have
heard from the White House that "Saddam Hussein is unlikely to

initiate a chemical or biological attack against the United States." Even more importantly, our intelligence agencies say that should Saddam conclude that a U.S.-led attack could no longer be deterred, he might at that point launch a chemical or biological counterattack. In other words, there is more danger of an attack on the United States if we launch a precipitous invasion. . . .

I do not know why the President feels, despite what our intelligence agencies are saying, that it is so important to pass a resolution of this magnitude this week and why it is necessary to go forward without the support of the United Nations and our major allies including those who are fighting side by side with us in the war on terrorism. . . .

But I do feel that as a part of this process, the President is ignoring some of the most pressing economic issues affecting the well-being of ordinary Americans. There has been virtually no public discussion about the stock market's loss of trillions of dollars over the last few years and that millions of Americans have seen the retirement benefits for which they have worked their entire lives disappear. When are we going to address that issue? This country today has a $340 billion trade deficit, and we have lost 10 percent of our manufacturing jobs in the last 4 years, 2 million decent-paying jobs. The average American worker today is working longer hours for lower wages than 25 years ago. When are we going to address that issue? . . .

[P]overty in this country is increasing and median family income is declining. Throughout this country family farmers are being driven off of the land; and veterans, the people who put their lives on the line to defend us, are unable to get the health care and other benefits they were promised because of government underfunding. When are we going to tackle these issues and many other important issues that are of such deep concern to Americans? . . .

[L]et me give five reasons why I am opposed to giving the President a blank check to launch a unilateral invasion and occupation of Iraq and why I will vote against this resolution. One, I have not heard any estimates of how many young American men and women might die in such a war or how many tens of thousands of women and children in Iraq might also be killed. . . . War must be the last recourse in international relations, not the first. Second, I am deeply concerned about the precedent that a unilateral invasion of Iraq could establish in terms of international law and the role of the United Nations. If President Bush believes that the U.S. can go to war at any time against any nation, what moral or legal objection could our government raise if another country chose to do the same thing?

Third, the United States is now involved in a very difficult war against international terrorism as we learned tragically on September 11. . . . An attack on Iraq at this time would seriously jeopardize, if not destroy, the global counterterrorist campaign we have undertaken. . . .

[A]t a time when this country has a $6 trillion national debt and a growing deficit, we should be clear that a war and a long-term American occupation of Iraq could be extremely expensive. . . .

I am concerned about the problems of so-called unintended consequences. Who will govern Iraq when Saddam Hussein is removed and what role will the U.S. play in ensuing a civil war that could develop in that country? Will moderate governments in the region who have large Islamic fundamentalist populations be overthrown and replaced by extremists? Will the bloody conflict between Israel and the Palestinian Authority be exacerbated? And these are just a few of the questions that remain unanswered.

If a unilateral American invasion of Iraq is not the best approach, what should we do? In my view, the U.S. must work with the United Nations to make certain within clearly defined timelines that the U.N. inspectors are allowed to do their jobs. These inspectors should undertake an unfettered search for Iraqi weapons of mass destruction and destroy them when found, pursuant to past U.N. resolutions. If Iraq resists inspection and elimination of stockpiled weapons, we should stand ready to assist the U.N. in forcing compliance.

Bernie's Senate floor speech decrying wasteful Pentagon spending, December 19, 2013[57]

The waste at the Pentagon is rampant, and we can go on for many hours just documenting the waste, but let me give just a few of the kinds of waste that the Pentagon regularly engages in. These are just a very few examples.

In July 2013 the Pentagon decided to build a 64,000-square-foot command headquarters for the U.S. military in Afghanistan that will not be utilized or even occupied. Even though the $34 million project was deemed unwanted by military commanders 3 years ago, the military still moved ahead with construction. The Pentagon has been paying contractor Boeing more than $3,357 for a piece of hardware they could have purchased from their own hardware store, the Defense Logistics Agency, for $15.42. It seems to me it would be a pretty good deal to get a product for $15 that you are paying over $3,000 for, but that is the way the Pentagon runs.

[Defense companies] make sure they have military contracts all over the country. So then any member of Congress who stands up and says "Well, maybe we don't have to spend $600 billion on the military." They get letters from people working in the military industry in their own state.

When we have this bloated and huge military budget, there are people who are talking about massive cuts in food stamps, massive cuts in education, massive cuts in affordable housing, cuts in Social Security, cuts in Medicare, cuts in Medicaid. I would argue very strongly that before we cut from the elderly and the children and the sick and the poor, maybe we take a hard look at this bloated military budget. . . .

It would seem to me that it is important we get our priorities straight. One of the priorities we should be getting straight is that we cannot give the Department of Defense all they want. It is time to take a very hard look at that budget in a way we have not done up to this point.

In 1988, when he endorsed Jesse Jackson in the presidential primaries, Sanders supported Jackson's Middle East views and criticized Israel's treatment of Palestinians. Here is a portion of that statement.[58]   —J.T.

The United States of America is pouring billions of dollars into arms and into other types of aid in the Middle East. Has the United States of America used its clout, the tremendous clout that it has by providing all kinds of aid to the Middle East, to demand that these countries sit down and talk about a reasonable settlement which will guarantee Israel's sovereignty, which must be guaranteed, but will begin to deal with the rights of Palestinian refugees . . . you have the ability when you are the United States of America, which is supporting the armies of the Middle East, to demand that these people sit down and support a reasonable settlement. . . . Or else you cut off arms. . . . If the United States goes into the Middle East and demands a reasonable, a responsible, and a peaceful solution to the conflict that has gone there because of its clout because of the tremendous amounts of money that it is pouring into that region I think we can do it. . . . It goes without saying. Soldiers of any nation especially an occupying power are not allowed under any moral code to break the arms and legs of people.

Bernie Facts

- When he was in the House, Bernie voted in 1991 against the resolution authorizing US military action in the Persian Gulf War.

- Bernie voted against authorizing the Iraq War in October 2002, calling it "one of the worst foreign policy fiascoes in modern American history" and noting that it "fomented the Islamic State terrorist group that plagues the Middle East today."

- He has repeatedly called for cuts in Pentagon budgets in order to fund social needs.

17

Foreign Trade

Deals That Protect People and the Planet, Not Corporations

So, what are they doing to the middle class in America? They are slowly but surely shrinking and enabling the shrinkage of the middle class of America. Free doesn't bring the standard of these other countries up. It's just cheaper labor and you see CEOs getting these huge bonuses.

—Stacy Bruenig, Gresham, Oregon[59]

Sanders has been one of the leading opponents of so-called free-trade agreements, which have cost the country millions of middle-class jobs and led to a decline in wages. He has been consistent, too. When he was in the House, he opposed the North American Free Trade Agreement (NAFTA) being pushed by President Bill Clinton, and he is now leading the opposition to the Trans-Pacific Partnership (TPP), a massive new corporate-backed agreement covering twelve nations in Asia. He sees all these agreements as benefiting big corporations, Wall Street, and the pharmaceutical industry, but not workers.   —J.T.

From Bernie's marathon Senate floor speech, December 10, 2010[60]

I returned from a trip to Vietnam last year, a beautiful country. People there work for 25, 30 cents an hour. Sometimes when you go to a store, you may see a shirt made in Bangladesh. That shirt, in all likelihood, is made by a young girl who came in from the countryside to one of the factories there. The good news is that in Bangladesh, the minimum wage was doubled. It went from 11 cents an hour to 23 cents an hour.

Are American workers going to be able to compete against desperate people who make 23 cents an hour?

I was in China a number of years ago and as part of a congressional delegation we went to visit Walmart in China. The Walmart store, amazingly enough, looked a lot like Walmart in America—different products, but it looked like the same style. You walk up and down the aisles and you see all these American products. I remember Wilson basketballs, Procter & Gamble soap products—different products there for the Chinese, but a lot of the products were American products. They looked pretty familiar.

I asked the guy who was there with us who was, I believe, the head of Walmart Asia—the guy in charge of all the Walmarts in Asia—I asked him a simple question: Tell me, how many of these American company products are actually manufactured in the United States?

He was a little bit sheepish and a little bit hesitant and he said: Well, about 1 percent. Obviously, what everybody knew, it is a lot cheaper for the American companies to set up plants in China, hire Chinese workers at 50 cents an hour, 75 cents an hour, whatever it is, and have them build the product for the Chinese markets than it is to pay American workers $15 an hour, $20 an hour, provide health insurance, deal with the union, deal with the environment. That is not a great revelation. I think anybody could have figured that one out. But the big money interests around here pushed it and Congress and President Clinton, at that time, signed it and we were off and running.

So my view—and I think it reflects the views of the American people—is that of course we want to see the people of Bangladesh and the people of China do well. But they do not have to do well at the expense of the American middle class. We do not have to engage in a race to the bottom. Our goal is to bring them up, not us down. But one of the results of our disastrous trade policies is that in many instances wages in the United States have gone down.

Tom Donohue is the president and CEO of the U.S. Chamber of Commerce. He got a lot of publicity during the last election because the Chamber of Commerce became the funnel for a lot of money that went into campaigns around the country. All the rich folks and billionaires gave money to the Chamber of Commerce, and they were able to elect candidates who were sympathetic to their point of view.

Let's find out what their point of view is. This is a quote going back to 2004: "One job sent overseas, if it happens to be my job, is one too many. But the benefit of offshoring jobs outweighs the cost."

That was Tom Donohue, president and CEO of the largest business organization in America. They are in favor of offshoring American jobs. They think it is a good idea. They understand that if corporations throw American workers out on the street and go to China and pay people there pennies an hour, it will make more profits. Give them credit. They are upfront about it. We don't care about the United States of America. We don't care about young people. We don't care about the future of this country. The future of the world is in China.

Bernie has always underscored that bad trade deals didn't make jobs vanish into thin air. Big corporations moved those jobs to low-wage countries.   —J.T.

From Bernie's marathon
Senate floor speech, December 10, 2010[61]

Some shut down for a variety of reasons. But others shut down because we have trade laws that say you have to be a moron not to shut down in America because if you go to China, go to Vietnam, go to Mexico, go to a developing country, you pay workers there a fraction of what you are paying the workers in America. Why wouldn't you go? Then you bring your products right back into this country.

A couple weeks ago, my wife and I did some Christmas shopping. It is very hard to find a product manufactured in the United States of America. You do not have to have a Ph.D. in economics to understand we are not going to have a strong economy unless we have a strong manufacturing capability, unless companies are reinvesting in

Colorado or Vermont, creating good jobs here. You do not have an economic future when virtually everything you are buying is coming from China or another country.

We are not just talking about low-end products. These are not sneakers or a pair of pants. This is increasingly high-tech stuff. We are forfeiting our future as a great economic nation unless we rebuild our industrial base and unless we create millions and millions of jobs producing the goods and the products we consume. We cannot continue to just purchase products from the rest of the world.

When we had a manufacturing base in America in the 1940s, 1950s, 1960s, you could graduate high school and go out and get a job in a factory. Was it a glamorous job? No. Was it a hard job? Yes. Was it a dirty job? In some cases. But if you worked in manufacturing, and especially if you had a union behind you, the likelihood is you earned wages to take your family into the middle class, you had decent health care coverage, and you might even have a strong pension.

Where are all those jobs now? During the Bush years alone, we went from 19 million jobs in manufacturing to 12 million jobs, a horrendous loss of manufacturing jobs. Today, what are your options? You can get a minimum wage job at McDonald's or maybe at Walmart, where benefits are minimal or nonexistent. That is a significant transition of the American economy.

We have seen the auto companies, Chrysler and others, starting to rehire. [But] the wages of the new workers who are being hired are 50 percent of the wages of the older workers in the plant. You are going to have workers working side by side, where an older worker who has been there for years is making $25, $28 an hour, and right next to him a new hire is making $14 an hour. If you understand that the automobile industry was perhaps the gold standard for manufacturing in America, what do you think is going to happen to the wages of blue-collar workers in the future?

If all you can get with a union behind you in automobile manufacturing is $14 an hour today, what are you going to make in Colorado or in Vermont? Are you going to make $10 an hour or $11 an hour? Is that enough money on which to raise a family? Are you going to have any benefits?

From Bernie's Senate floor speech opposing trade deals with Korea, Columbia, and Panama, October 12, 2011[62]

One of the major reasons why the middle class in America is disappearing and why poverty is increasing and why the gap between the very wealthy and everybody else is growing wider is directly related to our disastrous, unfettered free-trade policy. If the United States is to remain a major industrial power, producing real products and creating good-paying jobs, we cannot continue the failed, unfettered free-trade policies that have been in existence for the last 30 years.

We need to develop trade policies—I know this is a radical idea—that work for working people and not just the CEOs of large corporations. What we must do is rebuild our manufacturing sector and once again create millions of good-paying jobs where workers are producing real products made in the United States of America.

Over the last decade, more than 50,000 manufacturing plants in this country have shut down. Let me repeat that. In the last decade, more than 50,000 factories in this country have shut down. Over 5.5 million factory jobs have disappeared.

Back in 1970, 25 percent of all jobs in the United States were manufacturing jobs, often paying workers a living wage, decent benefits, pensions. Today, that figure is down to just 9 percent.

In July of 2000, there were 17.3 million manufacturing workers in this country. Today, there are only 11.7 million. . . .

I was in the House of Representatives when PNTR with China was passed. I can remember all of the fine speeches from the President on down, Republicans, Democrats. Permanent normal trade relations with China is going to open up that great market, going to create millions of jobs in America. It was not true. Free trade with China ended up costing us 2.8 million jobs. You don't have to be an economist to understand that; all you have to do is walk into any department store in America and buy a product. . . .

We all now understand what that trade agreement was about. It was not to open markets in China for American products, it was to open China so corporations in this country could shut down here, throw American workers out on the street, and move there in order to pay workers pennies an hour. That is what those trade agreements are about. There is no doubt in my mind that—certainly to a much lesser degree because they are smaller trade agreements—trade agreements with Korea, Panama, and Colombia will continue that same process. . . .

What we have here is that key advocates for continuing this disastrous trade policy are precisely the people who have been slashing jobs in America, closing down factories, and hiring people abroad. And I would suggest that Members of the Senate might want to think twice about listening to the advice of people who have been laying off millions of American workers. . . .

During the Clinton administration, we were told by Republicans and Democrats and then-President Clinton that NAFTA would create 100,000 American jobs over a 2-year period. That is what we were told about NAFTA. Well, results are in on NAFTA. Instead of creating 100,000 American jobs, the Economic Policy Institute has found that NAFTA destroyed more than 682,000 American jobs, including the loss of 150,000 computer and electronic jobs. . . .

The Economic Policy Institute has estimated that the Korea Free Trade Agreement will lead to the loss of 159,000 American jobs and will increase the trade deficit by nearly $14 billion over a 7-year period. Why would you want to go forward with those ideas? Why would you want to go forward with a trade agreement that will increase our trade deficit? . . .

Let me touch on one particular aspect of the Korea Free Trade Agreement that I find especially troubling and that I think the American people, to the degree they understand this and learn about it, will also find troubling; that is, this particular free-trade agreement will force American workers to compete not just against the low-wage workers in China or Vietnam or Mexico, they are going to be forced to compete against the virtual slave labor that exists in North Korea, the most undemocratic country in the world and a country itself whose government will financially benefit from this, with the dictatorship of Kim Jong Il. . . . Workers in North Korea are the most brutalized in the world, have virtually no democratic rights, and are at the mercy of the most vicious dictator in the world. But after the South Korea Free Trade Agreement is signed into law, the United States would have a new obligation to allow South Korean products to come into our country tariff-free that contain major parts made by North Korean workers who make pennies an hour. . . . These North Korean workers officially make a minimum wage of 35 cents an hour, but they actually make less than that. . . .

What about the Colombia Free Trade Agreement? It is understandable why the CEOs of multinational corporations would like this free-trade agreement. After all, Colombia is one of the most anti-union countries on the planet.

Since 1986, over 2,800 trade unionists have been assassinated in Colombia—more than the rest of the world combined. Think about it for a moment. If we found out that 50 CEOs had been assassinated in Colombia last year instead of trade leaders, do you think we would be on the verge of approving a free-trade agreement with that country? . . .

Lastly, let me say a brief word about Panama and the Panama free-trade agreement. . . . It turns out that Panama is a world leader when it comes to allowing wealthy Americans and large corporations to evade U.S. taxes by stashing their cash in offshore tax havens. The Panama Free Trade Agreement will make this bad situation much worse.

Each and every year, the wealthiest people in our country and the largest corporations evade about $100 billion in U.S. taxes through abusive and illegal offshore tax havens in Panama and other countries.

I feel very strongly that the policies we are debating today—trade policies with Korea, Panama, and Colombia—are nothing more than extensions of disastrous trade policies of the past. They should be defeated. We should come together and develop new approaches to trade, which will benefit all our people and not just CEOs or multinational corporations.

Bernie Facts

- Bernie was a key leader in the Senate fight against fast-track legislation and continues to be a leader in the fight against the Trans-Pacific Partnership (TPP).

- When he was in the House, Bernie led the opposition to, and voted against, NAFTA, which passed in 1993 with the full backing of President Bill Clinton and his administration.

- Bernie opposed free-trade agreements with South Korea, Colombia, and Panama,[63] and opposed the Central American Free Trade Agreement in 2005.[64]

18

Media
A Neutral Net, Making Sure All Voices Are Heard

*So many people around the county dislike this plan to allow
Comcast to gobble up so many more customers, including in
major markets like Los Angeles.*

—Hannah Sassaman, protest organizer at
Philadelphia rally, May 22, 2014[65]

For many years, Bernie has been one of the leading critics of the
growth of mega media conglomerates, the diminishing diversity in
the media caused by corporate consolidation, and the control of our
media by just a few global corporations. He has even held community
forums in Vermont with officials from the Federal Communications
Commission (FCC) to talk about the impact of rule changes that
affect the concentration of media ownership. —J.T.

From Bernie's House floor speech opposing the FCC's attempt to change rules on media cross-ownership, May 15, 2003[66]

The growing concentration of corporate ownership of media in the
United States is in fact one of the least discussed major issues in this
country because the media itself is in a major conflict of interest and
chooses not to discuss it. . . . Millions of Americans do not want to
see the handful of corporations who determine what we see, hear
and read become three, become two, become one perhaps as a result
of mergers and takeovers. . . .

   At issue now is the FCC's review of rules that seek to protect
localism so that back home they will have local news, that there
will be a local radio station telling them what is going on in their

community, that will preserve competition and diversity. These rules, among other things, currently limit a single corporation from dominating local TV markets. Do people want to live in a community where all of the local television stations are owned by one company? These rules that we have in place right now will prevent the merging of local television stations, radio stations, and a newspaper. Do people want to live in a community where one company owns their local TV station, owns the newspaper and owns radio stations? Do they think they are going to hear different points of view when that happens? . . .

I think sometimes when people turn on a television or they pick up a newspaper, they say, well, a company owns this newspaper, and a lot of companies put out different newspapers, different types of television stations, and so forth and so on. What people are not aware of is the degree, the number of separate companies that one large corporation owns. Let me start off with an example and go to Viacom. I suspect that most people have never even heard of Viacom. Who is Viacom? What is Viacom? . . . Viacom is a huge multinational corporation that owns TV stations, radio stations, TV networks, and many other media outlets. . . . When we turn on CBS network, that is Viacom. We turn on the UPN network, Viacom. MTV, Nickelodeon, TV Land, CMT, TNN, VH1, Showtime, Movie Channel, Sundance Channel, Flick, Black Entertainment, Comedy Central. One would think they are watching different companies. They are not. That is Viacom. They get off the TV now, drive into work, turn on the radio. There are 180 Infinity radio stations owned by Viacom. What about local television stations? We have got the big CBS. What about the local television stations? They must be locally owned. Wrong. We have 34 stations that Viacom owns in Philadelphia, in Boston, in Dallas, in Detroit, Miami, Pittsburgh, among other places. They are in radio. They are in television. But at least when I go [to] the movies I am getting away from this corporation, right? Not quite. When we watch Paramount Pictures, it is Viacom. MTV Films, Viacom. Nickelodeon, Contentville, the Free Press, MTV books, Nickelodeon books, Simon & Schuster. I am into music now. That is not Viacom. Wrong. Famous music publishers: Pocket Books, Viacom.

Star Trek franchise; Scribner's Publishers, Viacom. Touchstone, Spelling Entertainment, Big Ticket TV, Viacom Productions, King World Productions, all one company. One company. And they say it is not enough. We do not own enough media. We need to own more media. Break down the regulations so we can own more television stations, we can own more book publishing companies, and so forth. A very dangerous trend. . . .

The issue here is that in a democratic society, we do not know what goes on unless all issues of importance are discussed. . . . The reality is that in America we have lost several million jobs, decent-paying jobs in the last few years because of a disastrous trade policy where companies are throwing American workers out on the street and running to China. Have we seen much discussion about that on the TV? In the newspapers? I do not think so. . . .

I would remind my colleagues in Congress and all Americans that in the last days of the Soviet Union, which was a totalitarian society, people thought, well, I guess they had one newspaper and one television network, and that was it. It was a totalitarian society. That is wrong. There were dozens and dozens and dozens of different newspapers, different magazines, different television stations, all over the totalitarian Soviet Union. The only problem was that all of those television stations, radio stations, newspapers, and magazines were only controlled by either the government of the Soviet Union or the Communist Party. . . .

Let me say a word about News Corporation . . . it is owned by a gentleman named Rupert Murdoch, who was born in Australia, part of a newspaper publishing family in Australia. News Corporation today owns much of the media in Australia. Big deal. Well, they also own much of the media in the United Kingdom. They own a lot of the media in Eastern Europe. They are increasingly owning more media in China. And guess what? They already own a whole lot of media and other companies in the United States, and they want more. . . . So what you are looking at is one man who happens to be a right-wing billionaire controlling huge amounts of media all over the entire world, which makes him, in fact, one of the most powerful people in the world. . . .

How many people know that if you do that huge tax break, you are going to end up with a $10 trillion national debt that we are leaving to our kids and our grandchildren? Not a whole lot of discussion about that because Mr. Murdoch and the guys who make tens of millions of dollars a year want tax breaks for the rich. They want the American taxpayer to subsidize them, to give them billions of dollars in corporate welfare.

From Bernie's Senate floor speech about another important media issue, net neutrality, May 20, 2014[67]

What net neutrality means is that everyone in our country—and, in fact, the world—has the same access to the same information. Whether you are a mom-and-pop store in Hardwick, VT, or whether you are Walmart, the largest private corporation in America, you should have the same access to your customers.

Net neutrality also means that a blogger, somebody who just blogs out his or her point of view, in a small town in America should have the same access to his or her readers as the *New York Times* or the *Washington Post*.

If the FCC allows huge corporations to negotiate "fast-lane deals," then the Internet will eventually be sold to the highest bidder. Companies with the money will have the access and small businesses will be treated as second- or third-class citizens. This is grotesquely unfair and this will be a disaster for our economy and for small businesses all across our country. . . .

What does all of this mean in English? What it means is that when we talk about deregulating the Internet, we are talking about allowing money—big money—to talk, and allowing the big-money interests to once again get their way in Washington. That is very wrong. We cannot allow our democracy to once again be sold to the highest bidder.

I think all of us agree the Internet has been an enormous success in fostering innovation and enabling free and open speech across the country and throughout the world. We kind of take it for granted. . . . Unfortunately, these Republican Commissioners on the FCC want to fix a problem that does not exist. What they want is to change the fundamental architecture of the Internet to remove the neutrality that has been in place for decades—since the inception of the Internet—and to allow big corporations to control content online. . . .

Let me say the American people—people in Vermont and across this country—care very deeply about this issue. A little while ago, in advance of the FCC's vote, on the Internet I asked people in Vermont and throughout the country to share their views with me, to write to me and tell me what they thought about the attempt to do away with net neutrality, and I was blown away by the response we received. More than 19,000 people have submitted comments to my office so far, and what they are saying in statement after statement after statement is that the FCC has to defend net neutrality.

I think these 19,000 people represent the vast majority of the people in this country who understand how important net neutrality is, and I want to take this opportunity and a very few moments to share some of the comments I received through my Web site.

Anthony Drake of Moreno Valley, CA, said: Net neutrality is vital for a free and open internet, and the economic advantages that it has brought our nation and the world. Please work to reclassify ISPs as common carriers under Title II of the Communications Act.

William LaFrana of Versailles, KY, said: Everyone should have equal access to the Internet. The Internet was developed with taxpayer funding, and should not be held hostage to corporate piracy. . . .

President Obama himself has long been on record supporting net neutrality. In 2007, then-Presidential candidate Obama said: "What you've been seeing is some lobbying that says that the servers and the various portals through which you're getting information over the Internet should be able to be gatekeepers and to charge differential rates to different Web sites . . . so you can get much better quality from the Fox News site and you'd be getting rotten service from the mom and pop sites. . . . And that I think destroys one of the best things about the Internet—which is that there is this incredible equality there. . . .

Barack Obama was right when he said that, and I would very strongly urge the President to stand for what he said when he was campaigning for President and defend net neutrality.

I understand the FCC is an independent body, but the American people have spoken with a clear and unified voice that they want to maintain net neutrality. What is so frustrating for the American people is to elect a candidate—in this case President Obama—who campaigned on an issue and now see many of the FCC members he appointed moving in a different direction. It is simply not enough for the President to sit on the sidelines on this issue. We need him to speak out for net neutrality, as he did when he campaigned for President.

Let me conclude by simply saying the Commission will soon consider whether to reclassify the Internet as a so-called common carrier. Under this distinction, the Internet would be treated like other utilities. Being classified as a common carrier will mean Internet service providers must provide the same service to everyone, without discrimination. This is the only path forward to maintain an open forum, free of discrimination.

Bernie Facts

- Bernie has strongly argued to preserve net neutrality to ensure that regular people can have equal, affordable access to the Internet.

- Bernie has campaigned for more than two decades to ensure that big media corporations do not dominate the airwaves.

- Bernie has long fought to prevent monopolies from dominating the cable industry because those monopolies gouge consumers with unfair rate hikes virtually every year. Most recently, he campaigned against the effort by Comcast, the country's largest cable and Internet provider, to merge with NBCUniversal, one of the country's largest media conglomerates.

19

Government Oversight
What Is the Fed Doing with Your Money?

Before she could formalize her findings, Segarra said, the senior New York Fed official who oversees Goldman pressured her to change them. When she refused, Segarra said she was called to a meeting where her bosses told her they no longer trusted her judgment. Her phone was confiscated, and security officers marched her out of the Fed's fortress-like building in lower Manhattan, just 7 months after being hired.

—*ProPublica*[68]

Bernie has been a leading critic of the Federal Reserve Board, which, through its authority to set interest rates, has a major role in shaping unemployment levels (raising interest rates makes borrowing more expensive and thus usually depresses new hiring).

In a classic confrontation when he was in the House, Bernie confronted then Fed chairman Alan Greenspan on July 15, 2003: "I have long been concerned that you are way out of touch with the needs of the middle class and working families of our country; that you see your major function . . . in your position as the need to represent the wealthy and large corporations. . . . You don't know what's going [on] in the real world . . . the country clubs and cocktail parties are not real America. . . . You talk about an improving economy while we have lost 3 million private sector jobs in the last two years, long-term unemployment has more than tripled, unemployment has been higher than it has been since 1994, we have a $4 trillion national debt, 1.4 million Americans have lost their jobs . . . CEOs make more than 500 times . . . what their workers make. . . . I hate to see what would happen if our economy was sinking."[69]

Bernie continued his sharp oversight of the Fed in the Senate in the wake of the financial crisis, demanding to know which institutions received bailout money. When then Fed chairman Ben Bernanke appeared before the Senate, Bernie insisted on an answer: "I wrote you a letter and said, 'Hey who'd you lend the money to? What were the terms of those loans? How can my constituents in Vermont get some of that money . . . will you tell the American people to whom you lent $2.2 trillion of their dollars?'"[70] Bernanke refused to reveal the recipients. Which led to Bernie's amendment to have the first ever top-to-bottom audit of the Fed. The Bernie-fueled audit found, in July 2011, that the Fed had provided a whopping $16 trillion in secret loans to bail out American and foreign banks and businesses during the worst economic crisis since the Great Depression, but provided crumbs to small businesses.   —J.T.

From Bernie's Senate floor speech regarding his proposal to conduct a full-scale Government Accountability Office audit of the Fed, May 6, 2010[71]

What is bringing together some of the most progressive groups in the country with some of the most conservative groups, some of the most progressive members of the Senate with some of the most conservative? . . . At a time when our entire financial system almost collapsed, we cannot let the Fed operate in secrecy any longer. The American people have a right to know. . . .

Why was Lloyd Blankfein, the CEO of Goldman Sachs, invited to the New York Federal Reserve to meet with Federal officials in September of 2008 to determine whether AIG would be bailed out or allowed to go bankrupt? When the Fed and Treasury decided to bail out AIG to the tune of $182 billion, why did the Fed refuse to tell the American people where that money was going? Why did the Fed argue that this information needed to be kept secret "as a matter of national security"? . . .

When AIG finally released the names of the counterparties receiving this assistance, how did it happen that Goldman Sachs received $13 billion of this money; AIG, $182 billion; $13 billion going to Goldman Sachs—100 cents on the dollar of a company that was going bankrupt and that was bailed out. How is that—100 cents on the dollar? Not bad. . . .

Another question people might ask: Did Goldman Sachs use this money to provide $16 billion in bonuses the next year? Here you have Goldman Sachs getting $13 billion out of the $182 billion that AIG got, and the next year they are announcing $16 billion in bonuses. Did they use some of this money to provide those bonuses? . . .

As a result of the bailout of Bear Stearns and AIG, the Fed—and this is a beauty, this is quite something—the Fed now owns credit default swaps—listen up on this one—betting that California, Nevada, and Florida will default on their debt. So the Federal Reserve stands to make money if California, Nevada, and Florida go bankrupt. I suspect that the Senators from the great States of California, Nevada, and Florida would be rather interested to know that if their States go bankrupt, the Fed makes money. . . .

It has been reported that the Federal Reserve pressured the Bank of America into acquiring Merrill Lynch—making this financial institution even bigger and riskier—allegedly threatening to fire its CEO if the Bank of America backed out of this merger. When the merger went through, Merrill Lynch employees received $3.7 billion in bonuses. Was this a good deal for the American taxpayer? A GAO audit can help us find out. When the Federal Reserve provided a $29 billion loan to JPMorgan Chase to acquire Bear Stearns, the CEO of JPMorgan Chase, Jamie Dimon, served on the Board of Directors at the New York Federal Reserve. Let me repeat that. When the Federal Reserve provided $29 billion to JPMorgan Chase, the CEO of JPMorgan Chase served on the Board of Directors of the New York Fed. Did this represent a conflict of interest? . . .

Currently—and I think we have to appreciate this as well; we have to shed some light on these issues—some 35 members of the Federal Reserve's Board of Governors are executives at private financial institutions which have received nearly $120 billion in TARP funds, but we don't know how much these big banks received from the Fed. . . .

A number of observers believe—and the GAO can help us discover—the Fed provided zero interest loans to a large bank, which then took that money and bought government bonds at 3 percent. If that was the case, and I suspect it was, you are looking at a huge scam—when small- and medium-sized businesses needed the money. That was the intention of these loans. But I don't know how much of this was invested in growth bonds, you don't know, and the American people don't know. It is time we found out. . . .

The American people have a right to know when trillions of their dollars are being spent and who gets it. The American people have a right to know whether there are conflicts of interest. . . .

When the GAO released its findings, it was a stunning revelation of the Fed's operations and opened a new chapter in taxpayers' ability to understand where their money is going.   —J.T.

From the press release by Bernie's Senate office about the results of the audit of the Federal Reserve[72]

The first top-to-bottom audit of the Federal Reserve uncovered eye-popping new details about how the U.S. provided a whopping $16 trillion in secret loans to bail out American and foreign banks and businesses during the worst economic crisis since the Great Depression. An amendment by Sen. Bernie Sanders to the Wall Street reform law passed one year ago this week directed the Government Accountability Office to conduct the study. "As a result of this audit, we now know that the Federal Reserve provided more than $16 trillion in total financial assistance to some of the largest financial institutions and corporations in the United States and throughout the world," said Sanders. "This is a clear case of socialism for the rich and rugged, you're-on-your-own individualism for everyone else."

Among the investigation's key findings is that the Fed unilaterally provided trillions of dollars in financial assistance to foreign banks and corporations from South Korea to Scotland, according to the GAO report. "No agency of the United States government should be allowed to bail out a foreign bank or corporation without the direct approval of Congress and the president," Sanders said.

The non-partisan, investigative arm of Congress also determined that the Fed lacks a comprehensive system to deal with conflicts of interest, despite the serious potential for abuse. In fact, according to the report, the Fed provided conflict of interest waivers to employees and private contractors so they could keep investments in the same financial institutions and corporations that were given emergency loans.

For example, the CEO of JPMorgan Chase served on the New York Fed's board of directors at the same time that his bank received more than $390 billion in financial assistance from the Fed. Moreover, JPMorgan Chase served as one of the clearing banks for the Fed's emergency lending programs.

In another disturbing finding, the GAO said that on Sept. 19, 2008, William Dudley, who is now the New York Fed president, was granted a waiver to let him keep investments in AIG and General Electric at the same time AIG and GE were given bailout funds. One reason the Fed did not make Dudley sell his holdings, according to the audit, was that it might have created the appearance of a conflict of interest.

To Sanders, the conclusion is simple. "No one who works for a firm receiving direct financial assistance from the Fed should be allowed to sit on the Fed's board of directors or be employed by the Fed," he said.

The investigation also revealed that the Fed outsourced most of its emergency lending programs to private contractors, many of which also were recipients of extremely low-interest and then-secret loans.

Bernie Facts

- Bernie has repeatedly demanded that the Federal Reserve focus its efforts on reducing unemployment and creating jobs, criticizing Fed leader after Fed leader for being out of touch with the real lives of American workers.

- Bernie successfully pushed for a thorough audit of the Fed to expose which banks and corporations received low-interest taxpayer money; the audit revealed startling conflicts of interest and the doling out of trillions of dollars to big banks.

- Bernie opposed the reappointment of Fed chairman Ben Bernanke in 2009 in an effort to highlight the Fed's role in bailing out Wall Street firms and banks at the expense of regular workers.

20

Personal Liberty
Freedom and Unity

What the government used to be able to do because they had probable cause you were engaged in some wrongdoing they can do now without a warrant, without probable cause, without any idea of wrongdoing. That is a radical transformation in the relationship of we the people to the government.

—David Cole, professor, Georgetown University
Law School, from a February 2014 forum on the
National Security Agency and surveillance[73]

Bernie has been a strong advocate for personal liberty and freedom from government surveillance. He has repeatedly warned of the dangers posed by the National Security Agency's unlawful snooping into people's phone calls and the information they view or collect. He has also had a clear voice on issues of gun violence. He points out that people in Vermont who hunt are doing so as law-abiding citizens who are not any threat to others. At the same time, he has been a strong believer in taking steps to end wanton violence in America, supporting a ban on semi-automatic weapons, instant background checks for gun owners, and the ending of loopholes that have allowed guns to be bought at gun shows where buyers and sellers skirt commonsense regulations.   —J.T.

—On the Surveillance State—
Bernie's statement after voting against
a controversial domestic spying bill, June 2, 2015[74]

We must keep our country safe and protect ourselves from terrorists but we can do that without undermining the constitutional and privacy rights which make us a free nation. This is not just the government. It's corporate America too. Technology has significantly outpaced public policy. There is a huge amount of information being collected on our individual lives ranging from where we go to the books we buy and the magazines we read. . . . There are still too many opportunities for the government to collect information on innocent people.

—On Gun Rights—

From an interview with NPR, June 25, 2015[75]

My state has virtually no gun control but against strong opposition, I have voted for gun control so that should tell people around this country that I am prepared to deal with this issue. Second of all I think the people of Vermont and rural America are supportive of sensible gun control legislation. So the issue is, you know, what people say is, "I come from a rural state, which has no gun control, he's weak on gun issues." . . .

I can understand that if some Democrats or Republicans represent an urban area where people don't hunt, don't do target practice; they're not into guns. But in my state, people go hunting and do target practice. Talking about cultural divides in this country, it is important for people in urban America to understand that families go out together and kids go out with their parents and they hunt. And enjoy the outdoors. And that is a lifestyle that should not be condemned.

From an interview with the author, November 2013[76]

Vermont does have many gun owners who enjoy hunting, target shooting and other gun-related activities. But most people in Vermont understand that as a nation we must do everything we can to end the horror of mass killings we have seen in Newtown, Connecticut; Aurora, Colorado; Blacksburg, Virginia; Tucson, Arizona and other American communities. Clearly, there is no single or simple solution to this crisis. While the legislation [to expand background checks] recently brought forth in the Senate would by no means have solved all our gun-violence problems, it would have been a step forward, and that's why I voted for that legislation.

Bernie Facts

- Bernie has been a consistent opponent of broad surveillance laws, many of which came into effect under the PATRIOT Act. "All of us want to protect the American people from terrorist attacks but in a way that does not undermine basic freedoms," he said when voting against the act in October 2001.

- He subsequently voted against renewing the surveillance law in March 2006, and then as a member of the Senate voted against extending the PATRIOT Act in May 2011, when the extension passed 72–23.

- In a 1994 House vote, Bernie supported a ban on the sale of certain semi-automatic weapons, dubbed "assault rifles," to civilians. In the Senate, he has voted in favor of efforts to punish and deter firearms trafficking, as well as the regulation of assault weapons and large capacity ammunition feeding devices.

A Brief Biography
of Bernie

Bernie Sanders is no stranger to being the political outsider challenging an entrenched machine. Maybe it's due to the tenacity of a Brooklyn-born son of Polish immigrants who made ends meet as a writer, filmmaker, and carpenter when he arrived in Vermont in the 1960s. Or perhaps it's simply an extension of his belief that change comes from grassroots movements powered by people, like the civil rights movement in which he was active during the 1960s and 1970s. Whatever the reason, it's clear that Bernie does not give up and he builds on each election, which explains how he is now the longest-serving independent in the history of the Congress.

After moving to Vermont in 1964 following his graduation from the University of Chicago, he ran for governor and the US Senate in four elections, losing each time. But the message he carries in his current campaign for the White House was the same message he had in 1974 when he announced his candidacy for the US Senate: "I have the very frightened feeling that if fundamental and radical change does not come about in the very near future that our nation and, in fact, our entire civilization could soon be entering an economic dark age."[77]

He won election in 1981 as mayor of Burlington, Vermont, by just ten votes, defeating a longtime Democratic incumbent whom many believed was out of touch with working-class issues. During his four terms as mayor, Bernie spearheaded significant improvements in affordable housing and roads, improved the quality of the environment, and pushed for more progressive taxation, childcare, women's rights, and youth programs.

In 1990, after four terms as mayor of Burlington, he ran for the state's lone seat in the House of Representatives and won with 56 percent of the vote. In the House, he quickly became one of the most vocal progressives, leading campaigns in favor of taxing the rich, against the Iraq War, and against the North American Free Trade Agreement.

In 2006, he ran for the US Senate seat held previously by Republican-turned-independent Jim Jeffords, winning the seat with 65 percent of the vote. Though he won as an independent, he has caucused with the Democratic Party, giving Democrats crucial votes on progressive legislation in a chamber that has been narrowly divided since he assumed his seat. In addition, he has been given key committee assignments. When the Democrats were most recently in the majority, Bernie chaired the Committee on Veterans' Affairs at a time of great crisis in the management of the Veterans Administration (VA); in that role, he forged a bipartisan agreement for a huge reorganization and funding for the VA.

When the Democrats returned to minority status in the Senate following the 2014 elections, Bernie kept his seat on the Veterans' Committee but agreed to also be the ranking member of the Senate Budget Committee—a position that gives him a significant megaphone to articulate progressive priorities about how workers' hard-earned tax money is spent. He also serves on the Committee on Environment and Public Works, where he has continued to press his view that the United States must be a global leader on climate change, while the country also moves expeditiously to fix the nation's crumbling infrastructure. He has a voice on climate change via his service on the Committee on Energy and Natural Resources, where he has championed moving away from fossil fuels in favor of renewable power sources like solar and wind. He can also exert significant influence on workers' lives from his perch on the Committee on Health, Education, Labor and Pensions.

Acknowledgments

It is appropriate that Bernie Sanders' vision appears in these pages thanks to Chelsea Green, a Vermont-based, worker-owned publisher, which has published so many important, progressive books in an environment where independent publishers contend with mega corporations. When people buy this book, they are making a political statement—supporting, one hopes, the vision of Bernie Sanders but also supporting a publisher that values and lifts up independent voices. Margo Baldwin, Chelsea Green's president and publisher, did not hesitate to commit, enthusiastically and quickly, to the project. She and Shay Totten, the book's project editor, were superb partners in advancing the book from start to finish in a time frame that is a blink of the eye, in publishing terms. I also want to thank Michael Weaver, Chelsea Green's trade sales manager, Pati Stone, art director, and the rest of the production, sales, and marketing teams for their quick, dedicated, and skilled work.

Thanks also to Michael Briggs, who served as Bernie Sanders' Senate communications director before moving over to the presidential campaign as the chief spokesperson. Michael has been an invaluable bridge in the Bernie Sanders world. Jeff Frank, the current Sanders Senate press secretary, also provided leads to critical information.

Finally, a thanks to Bernie Sanders for being an authentic, honest voice willing to put himself on the line and to travel the length and breadth of the nation to ignite a political revolution that could change the course of history.

Notes

1. Donna Bailey, "Bernie Sanders' Presidential Campaign Announcement" (speech, Waterfront Park, Burlington, VT, May 26, 2015).
2. Bill McKibben, "Bernie Sanders' Presidential Campaign Announcement" (speech, Waterfront Park, Burlington, VT, May 26, 2015).
3. "Text of Bernie's Announcement," official campaign website, accessed July 27, 2015, https://berniesanders.com /bernies-announcement/.
4. J. Craig Anderson, "Thousands Expected to Greet Sanders in Portland," *Portland Press Herald*, last modified July 6, 2015, http://www.pressherald.com/2015/07/04/thousands -expected-to-greet-sanders-in-portland.
5. "Ten Fair Ways to Reduce the Deficit and Create Jobs," official senatorial website, accessed July 22, 2015, http://www.sanders .senate.gov/top10.
6. Julie Halpert, "The Healthcare Dilemma That Could Bankrupt Women," *Fiscal Times*, last modified March 25, 2013, http:// www.thefiscaltimes.com/Articles/2013/03/25/The-Health -Care-Dilemma-That-Could-Bankrupt-Women.
7. Bernie Sanders, "Statement on Supreme Court Decision Upholding Health Care Law," official senatorial website, accessed July 22, 2015, http://www.sanders.senate.gov /newsroom/press-releases/statement-on-supreme-court -decision-upholding-health-care-law.
8. Senator Sanders, speaking on SA 2837, 111th Cong., 1st sess., *Congressional Record* 155:191 (December 16, 2009): S13290–13294.
9. "Household Debt Continues Upward Climb While Student Loan Delinquencies Worsen" (press release), New York Federal Reserve, February 17, 2015, http://www.newyorkfed.org /newsevents/news/research/2015/rp150217.html.

10. Senator Sanders, speaking on S1373, 114th Cong., 1st sess. (May 19, 2015), official senatorial website, accessed July 23, 2015, http://www.sanders.senate.gov/download/051915 -highered/?inline=file.

11. Ben Adler, "How Bernie Sanders Can Be the Greenest Presidential Candidate Ever," *The Guardian*, last modified May 8, 2015, http://www.theguardian.com/environment/2015/may/08/how -bernie-sanders-can-be-the-greenest-presidential-candidate-ever.

12. "Climate Change & Environment," official campaign website, accessed July 22, 2015, https://berniesanders.com/issues /climate-change.

13. Senator Sanders, speaking on S.1, 114th Cong., 1st sess., *Congressional Record* 161:2 (January 7, 2015): S49.

14. Ibid.

15. Levy Morrow, "*The Ed Show* for Monday, June 22, 2015," accessed July 22, 2015, http://www.nbcnews.com/id/57533809/ns /msnbc-the_ed_show/t/ed-show-monday-june-nd.

16. Senator Sanders, speech, 111th Cong., 2nd sess., *Congressional Record* 156:163 (December 10, 2010): S8734–8744.

17. "Sanders Proposes Bill to Reduce Wealth Inequality," YouTube video, 11:19, posted by "Bernie Sanders," accessed June 25, 2015, https://www.youtube.com/watch?t=63&v=awXB5Ulaehk.

18. Michael Erman, "Five Years After Lehman, Americans Still Angry at Wall Street: Reuters/Ipsos Poll," *Reuters*, last modified September, 15, 2013, http://www.reuters.com/article/2013 /09/15/us-wallstreet-crisis-idUSBRE98E06Q20130915.

19. Senator Sanders, speech, 111th Cong., 2nd sess., *Congressional Record* 156:163 (December 10, 2010): S8734–8744.

20. New York State AFL-CIO, untitled post, *New York State AFL-CIO* (blog), accessed July 2, 2014, http://nysaflcio.tumblr.com /post/90555613832/senator-bernie-sanders-gets-it-the-attack-on.

21. Senator Sanders, speaking on HR 800, 110th Cong., 1st sess., *Congressional Record* 153:103 (June 25, 2007): S8338–8340.

22. Emanuella Grinberg, "Paid Leave Lets Dads Build Parenting Foundation," *CNN*, last modified June 16, 2013, http://www .cnn.com/2013/06/14/living/fathers-day-paternity-leave.

23. "Statement by Sen. Bernard Sanders on Family Values Agenda," official senatorial website, accessed July 22, 2015, http://www.sanders.senate.gov/download/061115-familyvaluesstatement.

24. Chris Johnson, "Sanders Touts LGBT Record in White House Bid," *Washington Blade*, last modified May 15, 2015, http://www.washingtonblade.com/2015/05/15/sanders-touts-lgbt-record-in-white-house-bid.

25. "United Against the War on Women," official senatorial website, accessed July 23, 2015, http://www.sanders.senate.gov/newsroom/press-releases/united-against-the-war-on-women.

26. Heather Boushey, "Social Security: The Most Important Anti-Poverty Program for Children," Center for Economic and Policy Research, March 28, 2005, http://www.cepr.net/documents/publications/social_security_2005_03_29.pdf.

27. Senator Sanders, speech, 111th Cong., 2nd sess., *Congressional Record* 156:163 (December 10, 2010): S8734–8744.

28. "Sanders Statement on Social Security Trust Fund Report," official senatorial website, accessed July 27, 2015, http://www.sanders.senate.gov/newsroom/press-releases/sanders-statement-on-social-security-trust-fund-report.

29. "Senator Bernard Sanders Floor Statement—June 27, 2012," official senatorial website, accessed July 27, 2015, http://www.sanders.senate.gov/newsroom/press-releases/senator-bernard-sanders-floor-statement-june-27-2012.

30. Jonathan Tasini, "Playboy Interview: Bernie Sanders," Playboy.com, last modified October 17, 2013, http://www.playboy.com/articles/bernie-sanders-playboy-interview.

31. Tim Dickinson, "Inside the Koch Brothers' Toxic Empire," *Rolling Stone*, last modified September 24, 2014, http://www.rollingstone.com/politics/news/inside-the-koch-brothers-toxic-empire-20140924.

32. "Sanders Files 'Saving American Democracy Amendment,'" official senatorial website, accessed July 27, 2015, http://www.sanders.senate.gov/newsroom/press-releases/sanders-files-saving-american-democracy-amendment.

33. Senator Sanders, speaking on S.J. Res. 33, 112th Cong., 1st sess., *Congressional Record* 157:188 (December 8, 2011): S8463–8464.

34. Bernie Sanders, "National Press Club Luncheon Speech" (Ballroom, Washington, DC, March 9, 2015).

35. American Society of Civil Engineers, "2013 Report Card for America's Infrastructure," InfrastructureReportCard.org, accessed July 12, 2015, http://www.infrastructurereportcard .org/executive-summary.

36. Senator Sanders, speech, 111th Cong., 2nd sess., *Congressional Record* 156:163 (December 10, 2010): S8734–8744.

37. Senator Sanders, speaking on SA 323, 114th Cong., 1st sess., *Congressional Record* 161:49 (March 24, 2015): S1472.

38. Senator Sanders, speaking on SA 23, 114th Cong., 1st sess., *Congressional Record* 161:14 (January 28, 2015): S568.

39. Jill Lawrence, "How Bernie Sanders Fought for Our Veterans," *Politico*, last modified July 2, 2015, http://www.politico.com /magazine/story/2015/07/how-bernie-sanders-fought-for-our -veterans-119708_full.html.

40. Annie Linsky, "Bernie Sanders' Surge Is Partly Fueled by Veterans," *Boston Globe*, last modified June 28, 2015, https:// www.bostonglobe.com/news/politics/2015/06/27/bernie -sanders-surge-partly-fueled-veterans/e1qNTpzFpIaoxIGK ygKa9J/story.html.

41. Senator Sanders, speaking on S. 1982, 113th Cong., 2nd sess., *Congressional Record* 160:33 (February 27, 2014): S1204–S1207.

42. *Burlington Free Press* Staff, "Sanders: Senate Opposes Cuts to Social Security, Veterans' Benefits," BurlingtonFreePress.com, last modified March 23, 2013, http://archive.burlington freepress.com/article/20130323/NEWS03/303230004 /Sanders-Senate-opposes-cuts-to-Social-Security -veterans-benefits.

43. Jonathan Tasini, "Playboy Interview: Bernie Sanders," *Playboy*, last modified October 17, 2013, http://www.playboy.com /articles/bernie-sanders-playboy-interview.

44. US Senate Committee on Veterans' Affairs "Senate Opposes Chained CPI Cuts to Social Security, Veterans' Benefits," *Veterans Advantage*, last modified March 22, 2013, https://www.veteransadvantage.com/va/benefitnews/senate-opposes-chained-cpi-cuts-social-security-veterans-benefits.

45. Pete Hardin, "Vermont Senator Bernie Sanders Targets Dean Foods, Dairy Antitrust," *The Milkweed* 361 (August 2009): 4.

46. Senator Sanders, speaking on SA 2276, 111th Cong., 1st sess., *Congressional Record* 155:120 (August 4, 2009): S8714.

47. Senator Sanders, speaking on SA 954, 113th Cong., 1st sess., *Congressional Record* 159:73 (May 23, 2013): S3731-S3732.

48. "DREAM Act Immigration Protest Shuts Down Street in Los Angeles," Rt.com, last modified August 3, 2010, https://www.rt.com/usa/dream-act-immigration-protest.

49. "Sanders Addresses National Latino Conference," official campaign website, accessed July 22, 2015, https://berniesanders.com/press-release/sanders-addresses-national-latino-conference.

50. Killer Mike, Twitter post, June 29, 2015, 11:04 a.m., https://twitter.com/killermikegto.

51. "Bernie Sanders Speech to National Council of La Raza," YouTube video, 23:52, posted by "Bernie 2016," July 13, 2015, https://www.youtube.com/watch?v=KgAwpb8rukk.

52. Bernie Sanders, interview by David Greene, *Morning Edition*, National Public Radio, June 25, 2015.

53. "Sanders: Take Down the Confederate Flag," official senatorial website, accessed July 23, 2015, http://www.sanders.senate.gov/newsroom/recent-business/sanders-take-down-the-confederate-flag.

54. "Youth Jobs Now," official senatorial website, accessed July 23, 2015, http://www.sanders.senate.gov/newsroom/video-audio/youth-jobs-now.

55. J. Craig Anderson, "Thousands Expected to Greet Sanders in Portland," *Portland Press Herald*, last modified July 6, 2015, http://www.pressherald.com/2015/07/04/thousands-expected-to-greet-sanders-in-portland.

56. "Flashback: Rep. Bernie Sanders Opposes Iraq War," YouTube video on official senatorial website, 5:36, posted by "Bernie Sanders," October 29, 2014, http://www.sanders.senate.gov /video/flashback-rep-bernie-sanders-opposes-iraq-war.

57. Senator Sanders, speech, 113th Cong., 1st sess., *Congressional Record* 159:181 (December 19, 2013): S9021–9022.

58. Zaid Jilani, "In 1988, Bernie Sanders Condemned Israeli Attacks on Palestinians as 'Reprehensible,'" *AlterNet*, last modified July 2, 2015, http://www.alternet.org/1988-bernie-sanders -condemned-israeli-attacks-palestinians-reprehensible.

59. The Oregon Fair Trade Campaign, "Faces of Free Trade and Job Loss: Confronting Oregon's Shifting Economy," accessed July 23, 2015, http://www.citizenstrade.org/ctc/oregon/files /2011/12/Faces_of_Free_Trade.pdf.

60. Senator Sanders, speech, 111th Cong., 2nd sess., *Congressional Record* 156:163 (December 10, 2010): S8734–8744.

61. Ibid.

62. Senator Sanders, speech, 112th Cong., 1st sess., *Congressional Record* 157:152 (October 12, 2011): S6423–6424.

63. Ibid., S6435–6438.

64. Bernie Sanders, "Sanders to Oppose Central American Free Trade Agreement (CAFTA)," *Vote Smart*, last modified January 14, 2005, http://votesmart.org/public-statement/86325/sanders -to-oppose-central-american-free-trade-agreement-cafta.

65. Meg James, "Comcast Investor Meeting Draws Protest," *Los Angeles Times*, last modified May 22, 2014, http://www .latimes.com/entertainment/envelope/cotown/la-et-ct -comcast-shareholder-meeting-20140522-story.html.

66. Congressman Sanders, speech, 108th Cong., 1st sess., *Congressional Record* 149:73 (May 15, 2003): H4179–4184.

67. Senator Sanders, speech, 113th Cong., 2nd sess., *Congressional Record* 160:76 (May 20, 2014): S3168–3169.

68. Jake Bernstein, "NY Fed Fired Examiner Who Took on Goldman," *ProPublica*, last modified October 10, 2013, http:// www.propublica.org/article/ny-fed-fired-examiner-who-took -on-goldman.

69. C-SPAN, "Bernie Sanders Blasts Alan Greenspan," *C-SPAN* video, 5:11, November 11, 2013, http://www.c-span.org/video /?c4472822/bernie-sanders-blasts-alan-greenspan.

70. C-SPAN, "Senator Bernie Sanders (I-VT): Where's the Money, Mr. Bernanke?," *C-SPAN* video, 5:39, May 14, 2015, http:// www.c-span.org/video/?c4537674/senator-bernie-sanders -wheres-money-mr-bernanke.

71. Senator Sanders, speaking on SA 3738, 111th Cong., 2nd sess., *Congressional Record* 156:67 (May 6, 2010): S3329–3332.

72. "The Fed Audit," official senatorial website, accessed July 23, 2015, http://www.sanders.senate.gov/newsroom/press-releases /the-fed-audit.

73. Anne Galloway, "At Sanders' Town Hall, Legal Experts Say NSA's Dragnet Spying Can Be Curbed Without Undermining Public Safety," VTDigger.org, last modified February 3, 2014, http://vtdigger.org/2014/02/03/video-story-sanders-town -hall-legal-experts-say-nsas-spying-can-curbed-without -undermining-public-safety.

74. "Sanders Votes 'No' On Domestic Spying Bill," official senatorial website, accessed July 22, 2015, http://www.sanders .senate.gov/newsroom/recent-business/sanders-votes-no -on-domestic-spying-bill.

75. Bernie Sanders, interview by David Greene, *Morning Edition*, National Public Radio, June 25, 2015.

76. Interview with the author, November 2013.

77. Tim Murphy, "How Bernie Sanders Learned to Be a Real Politician," *Mother Jones*, last modified May 26, 2015, http:// www.motherjones.com/politics/2015/05/young-bernie -sanders-liberty-union-vermont.

Index

FSC
www.fsc.org
MIX
Paper from
responsible sources
FSC® C013483

Chelsea Green Publishing is committed to preserving ancient forests and natural resources. We elected to print this title on 100-percent postconsumer recycled paper, processed chlorine-free. As a result, for this printing, we have saved:

155 Trees (40' tall and 6-8" diameter)
70 Million BTUs of Total Energy
13,396 Pounds of Greenhouse Gases
72,651 Gallons of Wastewater
4,864 Pounds of Solid Waste

Chelsea Green Publishing made this paper choice because we and our printer, Thomson-Shore, Inc., are members of the Green Press Initiative, a nonprofit program dedicated to supporting authors, publishers, and suppliers in their efforts to reduce their use of fiber obtained from endangered forests. For more information, visit: www.greenpressinitiative.org.

Environmental impact estimates were made using the Environmental Defense Paper Calculator. For more information visit: www.papercalculator.org.

WITHDRAWN

About the Author

Natasha Kraus

Jonathan Tasini is a writer, an organizational strategist, and an economics and political analyst. He is the author of *It's Not Raining, We're Being Peed On: The Scam of the Deficit Crisis*; *The Audacity of Greed: Free Markets, Corporate Thieves, and the Looting of America*; *They Get Cake, We Eat Crumbs: The Real Story Behind Today's Unfair Economy*; and *The Edifice Complex: Rebuilding the American Labor Movement to Face the Global Economy*, a critique and prescriptive analysis of the labor movement. He has been widely published, including in the *Wall Street Journal*, CNBC, *BusinessWeek*, *Playboy* magazine, the *Washington Post*, the *New York Times*, and the *Los Angeles Times*. He is the founder, editor, and publisher of "Working Life," a leading progressive blog on work and the economy. He served as president of the National Writers Union (UAW Local 1981) for thirteen years.

You can find him on Twitter at @jonathantasini.